The Gospel According to Matthew
Part Two

Matthew 17–28

Barbara E. Reid

with Little Rock Scripture Study staff

Little Rock
Scripture Study

A ministry of the Diocese of Little Rock
in partnership with Liturgical Press

Nihil obstat for the commentary text by Barbara E. Reid: Robert C. Harren, *Censor deputatus*.
Imprimatur for the commentary text by Barbara E. Reid: ☩ John F. Kinney, Bishop of St. Cloud, Minnesota,
August 30, 2005.

Cover design by Ann Blattner. Interior art by Ned Bustard.

 This symbol indicates material that was created by Little Rock Scripture Study to supplement the
biblical text and commentary. Some of these inserts first appeared in the *Little Rock Catholic Study
Bible*; others were created specifically for this book by Amy Ekeh.

1   2   3   4   5   6   7   8   9

Library of Congress Control Number: 2018956721

ISBN 978-0-8146-6433-9   ISBN 978-0-8146-6409-4 (e-book)

DIOCESE OF LITTLE ROCK

2500 North Tyler Street • P.O. Box 7565 • Little Rock, Arkansas 72217 • (501) 664-0340 Fax (501) 664-6304

Office of the Bishop

Dear Friends,

The Bible is a gift of God to the church, the people gathered around the world throughout the ages in the name of Christ. God uses this sacred writing to continue to speak to us in all times and places.

I encourage you to make it your own by dedicated prayer and study with others and on your own. Little Rock Scripture Study is a ministry of the Catholic Diocese of Little Rock. It provides the tools you need to faithfully understand what you are reading, to appreciate its meaning for you and for our world, and to guide you in a way that will deepen your own ability to respond to God's call.

It is my hope that the Word of God will empower you as Christians to live a life worthy of your call as a child of God.

Sincerely in Christ,

✝ Anthony B. Taylor
Bishop of Little Rock

TABLE OF CONTENTS

Wrap-up lectures are available for each lesson at no charge. The link to these free lectures is LittleRockScripture.org/Lectures/MatthewPartTwo.

Welcome

The Bible is at the heart of what it means to be a Christian. It is the Spirit-inspired word of God for us. It reveals to us the God who created, redeemed, and guides us still. It speaks to us personally and as a church. It forms the basis of our public liturgical life and our private prayer lives. It urges us to live worthily and justly, to love tenderly and wholeheartedly, and to be a part of building God's kingdom here on earth.

Though it was written a long time ago, in the context of a very different culture, the Bible is no relic of the past. Catholic biblical scholarship is among the best in the world, and in our time and place, we have unprecedented access to it. By making use of solid scholarship, we can discover much about the ancient culture and religious practices that shaped those who wrote the various books of the Bible. With these insights, and by praying with the words of Scripture, we allow the words and images to shape us as disciples. By sharing our journey of faithful listening to God's word with others, we have the opportunity to be stretched in our understanding and to form communities of love and learning. Ultimately, studying and praying with God's word deepens our relationship with Christ.

The Gospel According to Matthew, Part Two
Matthew 17–28

The resource you hold in your hands is divided into four lessons. Each lesson involves personal prayer and study using this book *and* the experience of group prayer, discussion, and wrap-up lecture.

If you are using this resource in the context of a small group, we suggest that you meet four times, discussing one lesson per meeting. Allow about 90 minutes for the small group gathering. Small groups function best with eight to twelve people to ensure good group dynamics and to allow all to participate as they wish.

WHAT MATERIALS WILL YOU USE?

The materials in this book include:

- The text of the Gospel According to Matthew, chapters 17–28, using the New American Bible, Revised Edition as the translation.

- Commentary by Barbara E. Reid (which has also been published separately as part of the New Collegeville Bible Commentary series).
- Occasional inserts 🔥 highlighting elements of the chapters of Matthew being studied. Some of these appear also in the *Little Rock Catholic Study Bible* while others are supplied by staff writers.
- Questions for study, reflection, and discussion at the end of each lesson.
- Opening and closing prayers for each lesson, as well as other prayer forms available in the closing pages of the book.

In addition, there are wrap-up lectures available for each lesson. Your group may choose to purchase a DVD containing these lectures or make use of the audio or video lectures online at no charge. The link to these free lectures is: LittleRockScripture.org/Lectures/MatthewPartTwo. Of course, if your group has access to qualified speakers, you may choose to have live presentations.

Each person will need a current translation of the Bible. We recommend the *Little Rock Catholic Study Bible*, which makes use of the New American Bible, Revised Edition. Other translations, such as the New Jerusalem Bible or the New Revised Standard Version: Catholic Edition, would also work well.

HOW WILL YOU USE THESE MATERIALS?

Prepare in advance

Using Lesson One as an example:

- Begin with a simple prayer like the one found on page 11.
- Read the assigned material in the printed book for Lesson One (pages 12–21) so that you are prepared for the weekly small group session. You may do this assignment by reading a portion over a period of several days (effective and manageable) or by preparing all at once (more challenging).
- Answer the questions, Exploring Lesson One, found at the end of the assigned reading, pages 21–23.
- Use the Closing Prayer on page 23 when you complete your study. This prayer may be used again when you meet with the group.

Meet with your small group

- After introductions and greetings, allow time for prayer (about 5 minutes) as you begin the group session. You may use the prayer found on page 11 (also used by individuals in their preparation) or use a prayer of your choosing.

- Spend about 45–50 minutes discussing the responses to the questions that were prepared in advance. You may also develop your discussion further by responding to questions and interests that arise during the discussion and faith-sharing itself.

- Close the discussion and faith-sharing with prayer, about 5–10 minutes. You may use the Closing Prayer at the end of each lesson or one of your choosing at the end of the book. It is important to allow people to pray for personal and community needs and to give thanks for how God is moving in your lives.

- Listen to or view the wrap-up lecture associated with each lesson (15–20 minutes). You may watch the lecture online, use a DVD, or provide a live lecture by a qualified local speaker. This lecture provides a common focus for the group and reinforces insights from each lesson. You may view the lecture together at the end of the session or, if your group runs out of time, you may invite group members to watch the lecture on their own time after the discussion.

Above all, be aware that the Holy Spirit is moving within and among you.

The Gospel According to
Matthew

Part Two

LESSON ONE

Introduction and Matthew 17–19

Begin your personal study and group discussion with a simple and sincere prayer such as:

Prayer

Loving God, as we read and study your living word, send us the Spirit of Christ, that we may faithfully heed his words and imitate his life.

Read the Introduction on page 12 and the Bible text of Matthew 17–19 found in the outside columns of pages 13–19, highlighting what stands out to you.

Read the accompanying commentary to add to your understanding.

Respond to the questions on pages 21–23, Exploring Lesson One.

The Closing Prayer on page 23 is for your personal use and may be used at the end of group discussion.

INTRODUCTION

Welcome to the study of *The Gospel According to Matthew, Part Two* from Little Rock Scripture Study. This volume will explore in depth Matthew 17:1–28:20, using the associated sections of Barbara E. Reid's New Collegeville Bible Commentary, *The Gospel According to Matthew*. The first half of this study covered Matthew 1:1–16:28 and included the appropriate sections of the same commentary by Reid.

In the first half of Matthew's Gospel, we became familiar with Matthew's unique presentation of Jesus as an authoritative teacher whose life and ministry fulfill the Scriptures. Jesus is Emmanuel, "God-with-us" (1:23; 28:20). We also learned that Matthew's Gospel reflects the situation of the evangelist's community. It seems that this primarily Jewish-Christian community was experiencing a painful separation from their Jewish counterparts in the synagogues, who likely felt that these Christians were dishonoring the covenant and unnecessarily fraternizing with Gentiles. Matthew wishes to be clear that faith in Jesus is compatible with faithfulness to the Jewish Law while simultaneously affirming the Church's mission to the Gentile community.

Matthew's Gospel begins with infancy narratives (Matt 1–2), which are followed by many teachings and miracles of Jesus. Five major discourses in Matthew's Gospel allow for organized, thematic collections of Jesus' teachings (Matt 5–7, 10, 13, 18, and 23–25).

As we move into the second half of the Gospel in this study, we will travel with Jesus to Jerusalem where he will teach with authority, be increasingly challenged by the religious leaders, suffer, die, and rise from the dead. Finally, the risen Jesus will commission his followers to "make disciples of all nations" and will promise to be with them always, "until the end of the age" (28:19-20).

JESUS AND HIS DISCIPLES ON THE WAY TO JERUSALEM

Matthew 17:1–20:34

17:1-13 The transfiguration of Jesus and the coming of Elijah

The question of Jesus' identity and what that means continues to loom large in this episode. On the heels of Jesus' teaching that he must suffer and die and then be raised up (16:21), the reader is given utter assurance that Jesus' execution does not mean that he is accursed (Deut 21:23) or in any way rejected by God. The brilliance of his face and clothing (v. 2) indicates his righteousness (see 13:43). The voice from heaven (v. 5) reaffirms the message heard at Jesus' baptism (3:17): he is God's beloved one. The instruction "listen to him" (v. 5) echoes Deuteronomy 18:15 and insists that Jesus is the correct interpreter of the Law and the Prophets, signified by the figures of Moses and Elijah (v. 3).

Matthew further highlights the portrait of Jesus as the new Moses with the details of the high mountain (v. 1; see also 5:1; 15:29; 28:16), Jesus' shining face (v. 2, like that of Moses after his encounter with God on Mount Sinai, Exod 34:29), and the overshadowing cloud (v. 5, like that which signaled God's presence with Israel in their sojourn to freedom, Exod 16:10; 19:9, etc.). Matthew specifically labels this experience a vision (v. 9), and the disciples react in

CHAPTER 17

The Transfiguration of Jesus

[1]After six days Jesus took Peter, James, and John his brother, and led them up a high mountain by themselves. [2]And he was transfigured before them; his face shone like the sun and his clothes became white as light. [3]And behold, Moses and Elijah appeared to them, conversing with him. [4]Then Peter said to Jesus in reply, "Lord, it is good that we are here. If you wish, I will make three tents here, one for you, one for Moses, and one for Elijah." [5]While he was still speaking, behold, a bright cloud cast a shadow over them, then from the cloud came a voice that said, "This is my beloved Son, with whom I am well pleased; listen to him." [6]When the disciples heard this, they fell prostrate and were very much afraid. [7]But Jesus came and touched them, saying, "Rise, and do not be afraid." [8]And when the disciples raised their eyes, they saw no one else but Jesus alone.

The Coming of Elijah

[9]As they were coming down from the mountain, Jesus charged them, "Do not tell the vision to anyone until the Son of Man has been raised from the dead." [10]Then the disciples asked him, "Why do the scribes say that Elijah must come first?" [11]He said in reply, "Elijah will indeed come and restore all things; [12]but I tell you that Elijah has already come, and they did not recognize him but did to him whatever they pleased. So also will the Son of Man suffer at their hands." [13]Then the disciples understood that he was speaking to them of John the Baptist.

The Healing of a Boy with a Demon

[14]When they came to the crowd a man approached, knelt down before him, [15]and said, "Lord, have pity on my son, for he is a lunatic and suffers severely; often he falls into fire, and often into water. [16]I brought him to your disciples, but they could not cure him." [17]Jesus said in reply, "O faithless and perverse generation, how long will I

continue

be with you? How long will I endure you? Bring him here to me." [18]Jesus rebuked him and the demon came out of him, and from that hour the boy was cured. [19]Then the disciples approached Jesus in private and said, "Why could we not drive it out?" [20]He said to them, "Because of your little faith. Amen, I say to you, if you have faith the size of a mustard seed, you will say to this mountain, 'Move from here to there,' and it will move. Nothing will be impossible for you."[21]

The Second Prediction of the Passion

[22]As they were gathering in Galilee, Jesus said to them, "The Son of Man is to be handed over to men, [23]and they will kill him, and he will be raised on the third day." And they were overwhelmed with grief.

Payment of the Temple Tax

[24]When they came to Capernaum, the collectors of the temple tax approached Peter and said, "Doesn't your teacher pay the temple tax?" [25]"Yes," he said. When he came into the house, before he had time to speak, Jesus asked him, "What is your opinion, Simon? From whom do the kings of the earth take tolls or census tax? From their subjects or from foreigners?" [26]When he said, "From foreigners," Jesus said to him, "Then the subjects are exempt. [27]But that we may not offend them, go to the sea, drop in a hook, and take the first fish that comes up. Open its mouth and you will find a coin worth twice the temple tax. Give that to them for me and for you."

continue

much the same way as Daniel did to his apocalyptic visions (Dan 8:17-18; 10:7-9).

The discussion about Elijah (vv. 9-13) reflects a debate about the correct interpretation of Malachi 4:5 (3:23 Hebrew), which speaks about the coming of Elijah before the Day of the Lord. For Christians this has taken place in the person of John the Baptist (see also 3:1-17; 9:18-26; 11:1-19; 14:1-12).

17:14-20 The power of little faith

The tragic situation of a child who suffers from what is probably epilepsy (the Greek word *selēniazomai* literally means "moonstruck") becomes an occasion for further training for the disciples. The father's plaintive "Lord, have pity" echoes the pleas of other sufferers in the Gospel (8:2, 5-6, 25; 14:30; 15:22, 25; 20:30-31). While the disciples have been given the authority to cure every disease and illness (10:1), Matthew has not yet reported that they were ever able to do so (cf. Mark 6:13, 30). Jesus' harsh words for the disciples echo those of Moses as he voiced his exasperation with Israel (Deut 32:5). Jesus redirects the disciples away from focusing on what they lack, toward claiming and exercising the power they do have with their little faith (see also 6:30; 8:26; 14:31; 16:8; 21:21-22). See 13:31-32 for the parable of the mustard seed.

17:22-23 Second prediction of the Passion

The reaction of the disciples to this second prediction of Jesus' death and resurrection is not denial, as in 16:21-23, but overwhelming grief. Their progress in comprehension and acceptance advances as they move with Jesus toward Jerusalem (contrast Mark 9:2).

17:24-27 The temple tax

This story is peculiar to Matthew's Gospel. The issue is the payment of a yearly tax of a half-shekel that was obligatory for all Jewish males over twenty years old (Exod 30:11-16). This served for the upkeep of the temple, as well as a sign of solidarity among Jews both within Israel and in the Diaspora. Controversy over this payment may have stemmed from disapproval over the manner in which the money was used by the Sadducees or the shaming of those who were too poor to contribute. Jesus' exchange with Peter makes it clear that as children of God, whose house the temple is, they are exempt from taxes for the temple. Nonetheless, for the sake of not causing scandal, Jesus pays the money. The fantastic detail of finding a coin in the mouth of a fish gives the story the air of a folktale.

18:1-14 Greatness in God's realm

The fourth great block of teaching concerns life in community. The first section (18:1-14) focuses on the need for humility and for the care of the most vulnerable. The second (18:15-20) outlines a procedure for reconciling aggrieved members of the community, followed by a parable (18:21-35) about unlimited forgiveness. While these teachings are addressed to "the disciples" (v. 1), the nature of the instruction is to those with leadership responsibility, not to the "little ones."

 The designation **"little ones"** is a favorite Matthean term for Jesus' disciples. It simultaneously denotes their subjection to outside forces that often oppose them and their status as servants rather than those who should "lord it over" others (Mark 10:42; cf. Matt 18:6, 10, 14, 42).

In the first part (vv. 1-5) Jesus teaches leaders to cultivate humility by consciously identifying themselves with the concerns of the least important in the community. Children are certainly valued in families, but they are the most vulnerable and the least able to contribute to the sustenance of the group, at least until they are older. A second way to exercise humility is by showing hospitality toward those who are "nobodies" (v. 5). Lavishing care on them with the same attentiveness and openness that one would show to an important guest is the way of true leadership. Finally, leaders must be wary of putting any stumbling block (*skandalon*, vv. 6-9) in the way of a "little one." The consequences for doing so are dire. Matthew does not spell out precisely who the "little ones" are. They may be new converts or those whose faith is not yet strong. At 10:42 they are Christian missionaries. One's treatment of "the least" is the basis for reward or punishment at the last judgment (25:40, 45).

A further lesson in prizing each of the "little ones" is presented in the parable of the shepherd who goes to extraordinary lengths to re-

CHAPTER 18

The Greatest in the Kingdom

[1]At that time the disciples approached Jesus and said, "Who is the greatest in the kingdom of heaven?" [2]He called a child over, placed it in their midst, [3]and said, "Amen, I say to you, unless you turn and become like children, you will not enter the kingdom of heaven. [4]Whoever humbles himself like this child is the greatest in the kingdom of heaven. [5]And whoever receives one child such as this in my name receives me.

Temptations to Sin

[6]"Whoever causes one of these little ones who believe in me to sin, it would be better for him to have a great millstone hung around his neck and to be drowned in the depths of the sea. [7]Woe to the world because of things that cause sin! Such things must come, but woe to the one through whom they come! [8]If your hand or foot causes you to sin, cut it off and throw it away. It is better for you to enter into life maimed or crippled than with two hands or two feet to be thrown into eternal fire. [9]And if your eye causes you to sin, tear it out and throw it away. It is better for you to enter into life with one eye than with two eyes to be thrown into fiery Gehenna.

The Parable of the Lost Sheep

[10]"See that you do not despise one of these little ones, for I say to you that their angels in heaven always look upon the face of my heavenly Father. [[11]] [12]What is your opinion? If a man has a hundred sheep and one of them goes astray, will he not leave the ninety-nine in the hills and go in search of the stray? [13]And if he finds it, amen, I say to you, he rejoices more over it than over the

continue

cover a lost sheep (vv. 10-14). Christian leaders are to emulate God's care for Israel (Ps 23; Isa 40:11) and Jesus' compassion for people who are "like sheep without a shepherd" (9:36).

ninety-nine that did not stray. ¹⁴In just the same way, it is not the will of your heavenly Father that one of these little ones be lost.

A Brother Who Sins

¹⁵"If your brother sins [against you], go and tell him his fault between you and him alone. If he listens to you, you have won over your brother. ¹⁶If he does not listen, take one or two others along with you, so that 'every fact may be established on the testimony of two or three witnesses.' ¹⁷If he refuses to listen to them, tell the church. If he refuses to listen even to the church, then treat him as you would a Gentile or a tax collector. ¹⁸Amen, I say to you, whatever you bind on earth shall be bound in heaven, and whatever you loose on earth shall be loosed in heaven. ¹⁹Again, [amen,] I say to you, if two of you agree on earth about anything for which they are to pray, it shall be granted to them by my heavenly Father. ²⁰For where two or three are gathered together in my name, there am I in the midst of them."

The Parable of the Unforgiving Servant

²¹Then Peter approaching asked him, "Lord, if my brother sins against me, how often must I forgive him? As many as seven times?" ²²Jesus answered, "I say to you, not seven times but seventy-seven times. ²³That is why the kingdom of heaven may be likened to a king who decided to settle accounts with his servants. ²⁴When he began the accounting, a debtor was brought before him who owed him a huge amount. ²⁵Since

continue

They are not to be like the shepherds that Ezekiel (34:12) denounces for placing their own welfare above that of the "flock." They are to seek out the "lost sheep of the house of Israel" (10:6). The emphasis in Matthew's version of the parable is not on the repentance of the sheep (cf. Luke 15:7), but rather on the urgent task of the shepherd who follows God's will and experiences great joy in finding the lost (vv. 13-14).

18:15-20 A process for reconciliation

This section presents steps to be taken in the community when one member sins against another. The first step is direct confrontation, begun by the one who is offended (v. 15) and approaches the other with a willingness to forgive. The best-case scenario is that this first confrontation brings about the needed repentance, and then reconciliation results. If it fails, however, the next step is to involve one or two others from the community (v. 16). The aim is to establish the truth, relying on impartial witnesses or facilitators. If this does not work, then the matter is brought before the whole community (*ekklēsia*, "church," used only here and in 16:18 in the Gospels). If that fails, then the person is to be treated like "a Gentile or a tax collector" (v. 17). It is not clear whether this means to exclude the person or to emulate Jesus' practice of befriending such people (see 8:5-13; 9:9-13; 11:19; 15:21-28).

Here Jesus may be advocating that Christians be willing to sit and break bread together, even while they are working toward resolving their differences. Note that Matthew does not indicate the nature of the offense. Such a strategy would not work for every kind of sin. Note that the whole community has a role in binding and loosing offenses (18:18), and the whole body is involved in praying for reconciliation.

18:21-35 Forgiveness aborted

The process sketched above is lengthy and arduous. Peter asks Jesus how often you have to do all this—as many as seven times? In biblical terms, seven is a perfect number, signifying here an endless number of times. Jesus' exhortation to forgive seventy-seven times (v. 22) contrasts with the threat of Lamech, who vowed vengeance "seventy-sevenfold" (Gen 4:24).

The parable plays out in three acts. In the first (vv. 23-27) a king decides to call in his "loan" (*daneion*), that is, the money due him from a slave who is a high-level bureaucrat (indicated by the amounts of money with which he deals, v. 24). This slave is evidently responsible for exacting tribute from other subjects. He builds networks and works the system to his and the king's advantage. The king, in a pure display of power, wants to collect ten thousand talents, approximately six to ten thousand days' wages. His purpose is to remind the servant of his subservience. The slave's response is exactly what the king wanted (v. 26). He does homage to the king and acknowledges his dependence and loyalty. The king is satisfied and returns him to his position. Word will spread both of the king's power and his generosity.

In the second act (vv. 28-30) the forgiven bureaucrat replicates the king's actions with his subordinates. This one owes him one hundred times less than the amount he owed the king. The point is not the difference in amount but that both are unable to pay. Although the second underling responds in exactly the same way his master did to the king, the latter carries through his threats with a vengeance instead of forgiving the debt.

In the final part (vv. 31-34) the fellow servants report everything to the king, who becomes enraged. If his servant has understood the meaning of his previous actions, then he should have replicated them. If the slave wants loyalty, adulation, and recognition of his power, the king has shown him how to exact it. Instead, he has shamed the king by not imitating him. He has said by his actions that the king's method of exerting power is not effective. If the slave thinks that physical abuse, debasing another, and brutal imprisonment are the ways to gain power, then the king will show him just that. The conclusion (v. 35) was likely added by the evangelist.

As with all metaphors, the king is both like and unlike God. Unlike the monarch in the parable, God does not work for his own self-aggrandizement, but for the well-being of all creation. But like the king, God, through Jesus, has graciously forgiven all debt of sin (for which Jesus teaches the disciples to pray in 6:12). The only response to such mercy is to let it transform one's heart so as to be able to act with the same kind of graciousness toward others. This kind of power is through vulnera-

he had no way of paying it back, his master ordered him to be sold, along with his wife, his children, and all his property, in payment of the debt. ²⁶At that, the servant fell down, did him homage, and said, 'Be patient with me, and I will pay you back in full.' ²⁷Moved with compassion the master of that servant let him go and forgave him the loan. ²⁸When that servant had left, he found one of his fellow servants who owed him a much smaller amount. He seized him and started to choke him, demanding, 'Pay back what you owe.' ²⁹Falling to his knees, his fellow servant begged him, 'Be patient with me, and I will pay you back.' ³⁰But he refused. Instead, he had him put in prison until he paid back the debt. ³¹Now when his fellow servants saw what had happened, they were deeply disturbed, and went to their master and reported the whole affair. ³²His master summoned him and said to him, 'You wicked servant! I forgave you your entire debt because you begged me to. ³³Should you not have had pity on your fellow servant, as I had pity on you?' ³⁴Then in anger his master handed him over to the torturers until he should pay back the whole debt. ³⁵So will my heavenly Father do to you, unless each of you forgives his brother from his heart."

VI: Ministry in Judea and Jerusalem

CHAPTER 19

Marriage and Divorce

¹When Jesus finished these words, he left Galilee and went to the district of Judea across

continue

bility and a willingness to forgo vengeance to work toward reconciliation. Those who do not learn to imitate godly ways in their dealings with one another will be treated by God in the way they have treated others.

19:1-15 Teaching on divorce and blessing of children

In his journey toward Jerusalem, Jesus takes the route along the eastern side of the

the Jordan. [2]Great crowds followed him, and he cured them there. [3]Some Pharisees approached him, and tested him, saying, "Is it lawful for a man to divorce his wife for any cause whatever?" [4]He said in reply, "Have you not read that from the beginning the Creator 'made them male and female' [5]and said, 'For this reason a man shall leave his father and mother and be joined to his wife, and the two shall become one flesh'? [6]So they are no longer two, but one flesh. Therefore, what God has joined together, no human being must separate." [7]They said to him, "Then why did Moses command that the man give the woman a bill of divorce and dismiss [her]?" [8]He said to them, "Because of the hardness of your hearts Moses allowed you to divorce your wives, but from the beginning it was not so. [9]I say to you, whoever divorces his wife (unless the marriage is unlawful) and marries another commits adultery." [10][His] disciples said to him, "If that is the case of a man with his wife, it is better not to marry." [11]He answered, "Not all can accept [this] word, but only those to whom that is granted. [12]Some are incapable of marriage because they were born so; some, because they were made so by others; some, because they have renounced marriage for the sake of the kingdom of heaven. Whoever can accept this ought to accept it."

Blessing of the Children

[13]Then children were brought to him that he might lay his hands on them and pray. The disciples rebuked them, [14]but Jesus said, "Let the children come to me, and do not prevent them; for the kingdom of heaven belongs to such as these." [15]After he placed his hands on them, he went away.

continue

Jordan River, as did most Jews, to avoid going through Samaria (v. 1). As at 16:1, rival religious leaders put a question to Jesus to test him (*peirazō*, as also 4:1, 3). Jesus' teaching on not divorcing was already introduced in the Sermon on the Mount (5:31-32). Now the question

centers on whether there are any exceptions (v. 3). The exchange is cast as a rabbinical debate, such as the one between the first-century rabbis Shammai and Hillel. The latter held that a man could divorce his wife even for spoiling a dish for him, whereas the former argued that only sexual misconduct was grounds for divorce.

In his reply Jesus first cites Genesis 1:27 and then Genesis 2:24, arguing that God's intention from creation is for man and woman to remain united. Jesus' opponents, also citing Scripture, come back with a text from Deuteronomy 24:1-4, where Moses permits a man to divorce his wife by handing her a written bill of divorce. Jesus distinguishes between God's positive command in Genesis, which reveals God's intent, and Moses' concession to Israel because of their inability to achieve the ideal. As at 5:32, Jesus characterizes divorce as adultery, unless the basis for separating is *porneia* (v. 9). The meaning of this word is not certain. It may refer to sexual misconduct, such as adultery or marriage to close kin, which was forbidden in Jewish law (Lev 18:6-18; see also Acts 15:20, 29). If it is the latter, then the question concerns some Gentile converts who wished to become Christian but who were in such forbidden marriages. Would they first have to divorce to enter the community?

The reaction of Jesus' disciples reveals the radical nature of his teaching. "It is better not to marry" (v. 10) is akin to the hyperbole in 18:8-9, which states that it is better to cut off a hand or foot or eye rather than cause a little one to sin. Jesus acknowledges that not all can accept this teaching. It has long been debated whether the saying in verse 12 refers to those who choose to remain celibate or to those who do not remarry after the death or divorce of a spouse. In Jewish tradition marriage was the norm, although some groups, such as the Therapeutae and the Qumranites, evidently practiced celibacy.

The reason why a Christian might make such a choice is for the sake of the mission. Many widows in the early church chose to live together and to devote themselves to ministry rather than remarry (see Acts 9:39, which may refer to such a situation, and 1 Timothy 5:3-16 for regulations regarding them). For women in Jesus' day, his stricter teaching on divorce may often have served a compassionate end, safeguarding women from being cast aside for no good reason and from being placed in a vulnerable position socially and economically. By the same token, painful decisions about divorce in a contemporary context must take into consideration Jesus' prime concern for the well-being of each person as a valued son or daughter of God in the community of believers.

In verses 13-15 the lens widens to the most vulnerable members in the family unit. When linked to the previous scene, Jesus' blessing and prayer for the little ones recognize that they may be the ones who suffer most when the parents are contemplating divorce. A reason why the disciples wanted to prevent the children from coming to Jesus is not given. In a pronouncement reminiscent of 18:3, Jesus speaks about their importance in God's realm.

19:16-30 Discipleship and possessions

The exchange between Jesus and the rich young man and the ensuing discussion with the disciples speak soberly about the obstacle that possessions can pose for discipleship. In Matthew's account (cf. Mark 10:17-31; Luke 18:18-30), the rich man asks Jesus about doing good, one of the evangelist's favorite themes (5:16; 7:17-19; 12:12, 33-35; 13:23, 24; 26:10). Keeping the commandments is a first step in doing good. The young man's question, "Which ones?" rings false, since all the commandments must be kept equally. Jesus' invitation to him to go beyond simply keeping the commandments and to "be perfect" (*teleios*, as also at 5:48) concerns becoming "whole" or "complete." As at 5:48, this is not an invitation for a select few, nor is it presenting a contrast between Judaism and Christianity. In the Old Testament, although riches are regarded as a sign of God's blessing (Deut 28:1-14), there are also the same dire warnings about the corrosiveness of riches (Ezek 7:19; Amos 6:4-8; Prov 15:16).

In Matthew's perspective, being a disciple of Jesus entails faithfulness to the Jewish Law

The Rich Young Man

¹⁶Now someone approached him and said, "Teacher, what good must I do to gain eternal life?" ¹⁷He answered him, "Why do you ask me about the good? There is only One who is good. If you wish to enter into life, keep the commandments." ¹⁸He asked him, "Which ones?" And Jesus replied, " 'You shall not kill; you shall not commit adultery; you shall not steal; you shall not bear false witness; ¹⁹honor your father and your mother'; and 'you shall love your neighbor as yourself.' " ²⁰The young man said to him, "All of these I have observed. What do I still lack?" ²¹Jesus said to him, "If you wish to be perfect, go, sell what you have and give to [the] poor, and you will have treasure in heaven. Then come, follow me." ²²When the young man heard this statement, he went away sad, for he had many possessions. ²³Then Jesus said to his disciples, "Amen, I say to you, it will be hard for one who is rich to enter the kingdom of heaven. ²⁴Again I say to you, it is easier for a camel to pass through the eye of a needle than for one who is rich to enter the kingdom of God." ²⁵When the disciples heard this, they were greatly astonished and said, "Who then can be saved?" ²⁶Jesus looked at them and said, "For human beings this is impossible, but for God all things are possible." ²⁷Then Peter said to him in reply, "We have given up everything and followed you. What will there be for us?" ²⁸Jesus said to them, "Amen, I say to you that you who have followed me, in the new age, when the Son of Man is seated on his throne of glory, will yourselves sit on twelve thrones, judging the twelve tribes of Israel. ²⁹And everyone who has given up houses or brothers or sisters or father or mother or children or lands for the sake of my name will receive a hundred times more, and will inherit eternal life. ³⁰But many who are first will be last, and the last will be first.

as interpreted by Jesus, which demands radical attachment to him. It is as difficult for a rich person to do this as it is for a camel to squeeze through the eye of a needle (v. 24). The popular interpretation that there was a gate so named in Jerusalem has no basis. Jesus' response to the disciples' astonishment (similarly, 19:10) is to refocus their attention on God's initiative and power with them, enabling them to do what is good—the question with which the rich man began (v. 16). See also the beatitude of the poor in 6:3 and the admonitions that the heart lies where the treasure is (6:21) and that one cannot serve both God and mammon (6:24). The treasure to seek above all is the realm of God (13:44). The theme of reward for disciples runs throughout the Gospel (5:12, 46-47; 6:1-6, 16, 18; 10:39-42; 25:21, 23, 34). Here the focus is eschatological. Disciples share in the glory and the final judgment by the Human One, as their self-emptying for God's realm has prepared them to receive the eternal inheritance God wills for all.

EXPLORING LESSON ONE

1. How does the transfiguration of Jesus assure the reader of the Gospel that although Jesus has predicted that he will suffer and die, he is not rejected by God (17:1-13)?

_____

_____

_____

_____

_____

2. In Matthew, Jesus urges his followers to use the faith they have, even if it seems "little" in comparison to the task (17:14-20). In what area of your life might Jesus be asking you to do the same?

_____

_____

_____

_____

_____

3. How do Jesus' disciples react differently to the second prediction of his passion than they did to the first (16:21-23; 17:22-23)? What might this mean?

_____

_____

_____

_____

_____

4. What are some of the lessons in leadership that Jesus teaches in 18:1-14? Have you seen examples of this type of leadership in the church, either among lay members or clergy?

_____

_____

_____

_____

_____

5. After reading the recommended process for reconciling a sinner to the community (18:15-20), what is your opinion of this process? What are some of the ways you have found effective in resolving conflicts within a community such as a family, friendship, or parish?

_____

_____

_____

_____

_____

6. What are two possible interpretations of Jesus' command to treat the unrepentant sinner "as you would a Gentile or a tax collector" (18:17; see also 8:5-13; 9:9-13; 11:19; 15:21-28)?

_____

_____

_____

_____

_____

_____

7. Have you ever forgiven someone over and over (18:21-22)? If so, who did it change more, you or the person forgiven? In what ways?

_____

_____

_____

_____

_____

8. Jesus appears to contradict a provision of the Mosaic Law that allows for divorce (19:3-9; see Deut 24:1-4). What scriptural basis does Jesus use for his teaching about the permanence of marriage? (See Gen 1:27-28; 2:18-24.)

_____

_____

_____

_____

_____

9. How would you explain Jesus' teaching on discipleship and possessions in 19:16-30? Why might following Jesus require giving up wealth and possessions?

_____

_____

_____

_____

_____

_____

CLOSING PRAYER

Prayer

"This is my beloved Son, with whom I am well pleased; listen to him."　　(Matt 17:5)

Lord Jesus, you are our Teacher, and we have listened closely to your teachings about humility, forgiveness, and the challenge of discipleship. Help us to live out these teachings in our lives, so we may love others with the love you have shown to us and willingly make the sacrifices you ask of us so we may follow you closely. Today we pray for all those who are part of our lives and in need of your loving care, especially . . .

LESSON TWO

Matthew 20–22

Begin your personal study and group discussion with a simple and sincere prayer such as:

Prayer

> *Loving God, as we read and study your living word, send us the Spirit of Christ, that we may faithfully heed his words and imitate his life.*

Read the Bible text of Matthew 20–22 found in the outside columns of pages 26–35, highlighting what stands out to you.

Read the accompanying commentary to add to your understanding.

Respond to the questions on pages 36–38, Exploring Lesson Two.

The Closing Prayer on page 38 is for your personal use and may be used at the end of group discussion.

CHAPTER 20

The Workers in the Vineyard

[1]"The kingdom of heaven is like a landowner who went out at dawn to hire laborers for his vineyard. [2]After agreeing with them for the usual daily wage, he sent them into his vineyard. [3]Going out about nine o'clock, he saw others standing idle in the marketplace, [4]and he said to them, 'You too go into my vineyard, and I will give you what is just.' [5]So they went off. [And] he went out again around noon, and around three o'clock, and did likewise. [6]Going out about five o'clock, he found others standing around, and said to them, 'Why do you stand here idle all day?' [7]They answered, 'Because no one has hired us.' He said to them, 'You too go into my vineyard.' [8]When it was evening the owner of the vineyard said to his foreman, 'Summon the laborers and give them their pay, beginning with the last and ending with the first.' [9]When those who had started about five o'clock came, each received the usual daily wage. [10]So when the first came, they thought that they would receive more, but each of them also got the usual wage. [11]And on receiving it they grumbled against the landowner, [12]saying, 'These last ones worked only one hour, and you have made them equal to us, who bore the day's burden and the heat.' [13]He said to one of them in reply, 'My friend, I am not cheating you. Did you not agree with me for the usual daily wage? [14]Take what is yours and go. What if I wish to give this last one the same as you? [15][Or] am I not free to do as I wish with my own money? Are you envious because I am generous?' [16]Thus, the last will be first, and the first will be last."

The Third Prediction of the Passion

[17]As Jesus was going up to Jerusalem, he took the twelve [disciples] aside by themselves, and said to them on the way, [18]"Behold, we are going up to Jerusalem, and the Son of Man will be handed over to the chief priests and the scribes, and they will condemn him to death, [19]and hand him over

continue

20:1-16 Justice in the vineyard

This parable and the previous episode conclude with the same saying about reversal (19:30; 20:16). This is a floating proverb that is tagged on to various New Testament passages in diverse contexts (see also Mark 10:31; Luke 13:30). It does not supply the meaning for the parable. In the story the first hired are paid last because the point of the story depends on their seeing what the last hired receive. The complaint of the workers in verse 12 voices what is so puzzling about this parable. Does not justice demand that those who worked more earn more? The vineyard owner has promised that he will pay what is just (*dikaios*, v. 4) and insists that he is doing no injustice (*ouk adikō se*, v. 13). He then asks, "[A]m I not free to do as I wish with my own money? Are you envious because I am generous?" (v. 15).

Two important points are made in the landowner's reply. If he is a figure for God, his actions show that God's generosity, which is not merited, is freely lavished on those most in need. God's generosity does no injustice, but neither can it be calculated or earned. The story *is* about people getting what they deserve: all have the right to eat for the day. From the position of the day laborers, who are on the lowest economic rung and who stand waiting all day (v. 6), wanting to work but not hired, the wage given them enables them to feed their family for one more day. Less than a denarius would be useless. From their perspective, those who were hired at the beginning of the day, though they have worked longer and harder, at least had the satisfaction of knowing all day that come sundown they would be able to feed their families. In God's realm, justice means that all are fed as a sign of God's equal and inclusive love; it does not mean getting what we deserve, either in terms of retribution for wrongdoing or recompense for good deeds.

The second point is that "evil-eye" envy is the most destructive force in a community. The question in verse 15 is, literally, "Or is your eye evil that I am good?" In a first-century worldview of limited good, anyone's gain means another one's loss. While the grumblers focus on their perceived loss, they miss the limitless goodness and generosity of the landowner. Linked with the previous discussion about the danger of riches, this parable challenges those disciples who have enough to meet their daily needs to reject acquisitiveness and attend to the needs of those who are in desperate straits.

20:17-28 To drink the cup

The third prediction of Jesus' passion is more detailed than the others and occurs as Jesus and his disciples near Jerusalem. In the first prediction (16:21-23) Jesus told his disciples that he would be killed at the hands of the elders, chief priests, and scribes. In fact, the Jewish leaders did not have the authority to carry out capital punishment (see John 18:31). Jesus will actually be handed over to the Gentiles (v. 19), who will put him to death (cf. the second prediction, where Jesus spoke in general terms of being betrayed into human hands, 17:22-23).

It is jarring to have the disciples bickering over the places of honor in the kingdom after this sober prediction. Matthew redacts the story (cf. Mark 10:35-45), so that the mother of James and John makes the request, thus softening the critique of the disciples and making their mother the ambitious one. It is ambiguous whether the other ten are indignant at the audacity of the request or whether they are upset that these two beat them to it (v. 24).

to the Gentiles to be mocked and scourged and crucified, and he will be raised on the third day."

The Request of James and John

[20]Then the mother of the sons of Zebedee approached him with her sons and did him homage, wishing to ask him for something. [21]He said to her, "What do you wish?" She answered him, "Command that these two sons of mine sit, one at your right and the other at your left, in your kingdom." [22]Jesus said in reply, "You do not know what you are asking. Can you drink the cup that I am going to drink?" They said to him, "We can." [23]He replied, "My cup you will indeed drink, but to sit at my right and at my left [, this] is not mine to give but is for those for whom it has been prepared by my Father." [24]When the ten heard this, they became indignant at the two brothers. [25]But Jesus summoned them and said, "You know that the rulers of the Gentiles lord it over them, and the great ones make their authority over them felt. [26]But it shall not be so among you. Rather, whoever wishes to be great among you shall be your servant; [27]whoever wishes to be first among you shall be your slave. [28]Just so, the Son of Man did not come to be served but to serve and to give his life as a ransom for many."

continue

 James and John, the sons of Zebedee, are part of the inner circle of the twelve apostles, along with Peter. They feature prominently in several passages of the New Testament, including the transfiguration story (Matt 17:1; Mark 9:2; Luke 9:28). Later Christian tradition identified this James as "the Greater." Interestingly, their mother—who is never named—features in several passages as well (Matt 20:20-21; 27:56).

The metaphor "cup" is used often in the Scriptures to speak of the suffering of Israel (Isa 51:17; Jer 25:15; 49:12; 51:7; Lam 4:21; *Mart.*

The Healing of Two Blind Men

²⁹As they left Jericho, a great crowd followed him. ³⁰Two blind men were sitting by the roadside, and when they heard that Jesus was passing by, they cried out, "[Lord,] Son of David, have pity on us!" ³¹The crowd warned them to be silent, but they called out all the more, "Lord, Son of David, have pity on us!" ³²Jesus stopped and called them and said, "What do you want me to do for you?" ³³They answered him, "Lord, let our eyes be opened." ³⁴Moved with pity, Jesus touched their eyes. Immediately they received their sight, and followed him.

CHAPTER 21

The Entry into Jerusalem

¹When they drew near Jerusalem and came to Bethphage on the Mount of Olives, Jesus sent two disciples, ²saying to them, "Go into the village opposite you, and immediately you will find an ass tethered, and a colt with her. Untie them and bring them here to me. ³And if anyone should say anything to you, reply, 'The master has need of them.' Then he will send them at once." ⁴This happened so that what had been spoken through the prophet might be fulfilled:

⁵"Say to daughter Zion,
'Behold, your king comes to you,
    meek and riding on an ass,
    and on a colt, the foal of a beast of
        burden.'"

⁶The disciples went and did as Jesus had ordered them. ⁷They brought the ass and the colt and laid

continue

Isa. 5:13). In 26:39 Jesus implores God to let "this cup" pass him by. Jesus then instructs the disciples on the manner of leadership they are to exercise. They are not to "lord it over" any others; rather, like Jesus himself, they are to serve the rest of the community. Jesus' service is service to the death, a giving of his life as ransom for all. The word *polys*, "many," does

not exclude anyone. It reflects a Semitic expression where "many" is the opposite of "one," thus the equivalent of "all." The notion of Jesus giving his life as ransom draws on the image of a slave who buys back his freedom for a price. These last verses of the Gospel are aimed at leaders who have some degree of power, privilege, status, and choice. Their choice to take the lowly position of service is liberating when accompanied by empowerment of those who are otherwise powerless. These sayings must not be used to reinforce the servitude of those who are enslaved in whatever way.

20:29-34 A final healing

This is the last healing story in the Gospel. It mirrors the one in 9:27-31, where two blind men also cried out to Jesus, "Son of David, have pity on us!" (see also 12:23; 15:22). After having instructed his disciples on servant leadership (20:25-28), Jesus demonstrates for them the kind of descendant of King David he is. As in 9:27-31, Jesus engages the two men in conversation; he does not merely touch them and keep going. Jesus treats them not simply as objects of compassion but with dignity, as people who are able to articulate their need (v. 32). These two who see and follow (v. 34) model the response needed of disciples as Jesus now prepares to enter Jerusalem as Son of David (21:9, 15) to begin the ordeal that will culminate in his reign with God.

JERUSALEM; JESUS' FINAL DAYS OF TEACHING IN THE TEMPLE

Matthew 21:1–28:15

21:1-11 Entry into Jerusalem

Jesus' journey to Jerusalem, begun at 16:21, climaxes with his enthusiastic reception by a very large crowd (vv. 1-11), and his action in the temple (vv. 12-17). Both scenes are eschatological in tone and are heavily interlaced with quotations from the prophets, so that the significance in terms of fulfillment of Scriptures is most evident. Jesus enters the city from the east. The Mount of Olives, according to Zechariah 14:4 is the place where the final eschatological struggle will take place. Matthew seems to speak of two animals (v. 2), but he is preserving the parallelism of Zechariah 9:9 (quoted in v. 5), which actually describes only one beast. The prophet tells of the Messiah entering the city "riding on a donkey, / on a colt, the foal of a donkey." Jesus' action is a parody of that of a conqueror over a vanquished city. The Hebrew word *hôšiʾânāʾ* means "save, please!" Here it is not so much a plea for help as an acclamation of praise. The shouts of adulation of the crowd (echoing Ps 118:26 in v. 9) contrast with the mounting antagonism of the Jewish leaders. The reaction described in verse 10, "the whole city was shaken (*eseisthē*)," points ahead to the aftermath of the death of Jesus, when "the earth quaked (*eseisthē*," 27:51).

 At the time of Jesus, Judaism was a religion of **sacrifice,** which was inextricably linked to the temple in Jerusalem. The rituals were prescribed by ancient scriptural directives and controlled by the various categories of priests who worked at the temple. Sacrifices included foods from the harvest for certain feasts or various animals, such as birds, sheep, goats, and cattle, depending on the purpose of the request. Sacrifices helped to make God's presence concrete. They included peace offerings, purification rituals, or rituals for atonement and forgiveness. Later, after the destruction of the temple in A.D. 70, Judaism became a religion of the word with a strong ethical emphasis.

21:12-17 Confrontation in the temple

In Matthew's account, Jesus' entry into Jerusalem culminates with his action in the temple (cf. Mark 11:15-19, where Jesus waits until the next day). Scholars still speculate on the nature of the abuse that Jesus was protesting. The interpretation of each evangelist differs slightly. In Matthew's account, Jesus

their cloaks over them, and he sat upon them. [8]The very large crowd spread their cloaks on the road, while others cut branches from the trees and strewed them on the road. [9]The crowds preceding him and those following kept crying out and saying:

> "Hosanna to the Son of David;
>   blessed is he who comes in the name of
>   the Lord;
>   hosanna in the highest."

[10]And when he entered Jerusalem the whole city was shaken and asked, "Who is this?" [11]And the crowds replied, "This is Jesus the prophet, from Nazareth in Galilee."

The Cleansing of the Temple

[12]Jesus entered the temple area and drove out all those engaged in selling and buying there. He overturned the tables of the money changers and the seats of those who were selling doves. [13]And he said to them, "It is written:

> 'My house shall be a house of prayer,'
>   but you are making it a den of thieves."

[14]The blind and the lame approached him in the temple area, and he cured them. [15]When the chief priests and the scribes saw the wondrous things he was doing, and the children crying out in the temple area, "Hosanna to the Son of David," they were indignant [16]and said to him, "Do you hear what they are saying?" Jesus said to them, "Yes; and have you never read the text, 'Out of the mouths of infants and nurslings you have brought forth praise'?" [17]And leaving them, he went out of the city to Bethany, and there he spent the night.

continue

interrupts the commercial activity in the temple area (v. 12). Buying and selling of animals was necessary for temple sacrifice. Doves were the poor woman's offering after childbirth (Lev 12:6-8; Luke 2:24). Greek and Roman coins had to be changed into Tyrian shekels, not because

The Cursing of the Fig Tree

[18]When he was going back to the city in the morning, he was hungry. [19]Seeing a fig tree by the road, he went over to it, but found nothing on it except leaves. And he said to it, "May no fruit ever come from you again." And immediately the fig tree withered. [20]When the disciples saw this, they were amazed and said, "How was it that the fig tree withered immediately?" [21]Jesus said to them in reply, "Amen, I say to you, if you have faith and do not waver, not only will you do what has been done to the fig tree, but even if you say to this mountain, 'Be lifted up and thrown into the sea,' it will be done. [22]Whatever you ask for in prayer with faith, you will receive."

The Authority of Jesus Questioned

[23]When he had come into the temple area, the chief priests and the elders of the people approached him as he was teaching and said, "By what authority are you doing these things? And who gave you this authority?" [24]Jesus said to them in reply, "I shall ask you one question, and if you answer it for me, then I shall tell you by what authority I do these things. [25]Where was John's baptism from? Was it of heavenly or of human origin?" They discussed this among themselves and said, "If we say 'Of heavenly origin,' he will say to us, 'Then why did you not believe him?' [26]But if we say, 'Of human origin,' we fear the crowd, for they all regard John as a prophet." [27]So they said to Jesus in reply, "We do not know." He himself said to them, "Neither shall I tell you by what authority I do these things.

continue

they lacked an offensive image, but because they had the highest silver content.

Matthew interprets Jesus' action (v. 13) by combining quotations from Isaiah 56:7 and Jeremiah 7:11. The first speaks of the messianic ideal of the temple being a perfect place of prayer for all peoples (though Matthew omits that last phrase; cf. Mark 11:16). The second

was a warning to the people of Judah, who continued trusting in the efficacy of temple worship while their deeds toward one another were rampantly unjust. Jeremiah warned that their corruption was defiling their "hideout," the temple, and predicted its destruction. In verses 12-13 Matthew's Jesus is a fiery prophet bent on rectifying abuse. In verses 14-17, unique to Matthew, Jesus is the compassionate healer of those who are least welcome in the temple (see Lev 21:18, where the blind and the lame are forbidden to offer sacrifices).

Jesus fulfills the messianic promise of Isaiah 35:5-6, where all, including those who are blind and lame, are healed and march exultantly into Jerusalem. Typically, the response to Jesus is divided. The leaders become indignant, while the children (see also 18:1-4; 19:13-15) sing "Hosanna to the Son of David" (see the use of this title in healing stories at 9:27; 12:23; 15:22; 20:30, 31). Jesus responds by quoting from Psalm 8:3.

21:18-22 The withered fig tree

This strange story may have evolved from the parable of the fig tree in Luke 13:6-9. Fruitful figs and vines are a symbol of peace and prosperity (1 Kgs 4:25), and Matthew frequently uses the metaphor "bear fruit" to speak of doing righteous deeds (cf. 3:8; 7:15-20; 12:33-37; 13:23; 21:19, 33-43). In the Matthean setting, there are strong eschatological overtones from chapter 21 forward. The time has arrived when there must be evidence of "good fruit," or else there will be destruction of the temple and condemnation of those who lead people astray (see also Jer 8:13; Hos 9:10, 16). The last two verses shift emphasis, so that the story becomes one about the power of faith (see also 7:7-11; cf. 6:30; 8:25, 26; 14:30, 31; 16:8; 17:20, where Jesus chides the disciples for their lack of faith). Jesus does not promise that the object of every prayerful request will be granted; rather, he assures believers that when they pray with faith in God's gracious goodness, God will always be with them (1:23; 28:20). God's power is at work in believers, even when they confront the most insurmountable obstacles.

21:23-27 The authority of Jesus

Throughout Matthew's Gospel, Jesus is portrayed as the authoritative teacher whom many people follow but whom the leaders reject. Now there are open confrontations between Jesus and the religious authorities. The chief priests and elders (v. 23) are the leading opponents in the passion narrative (the Pharisees drop out of view after chapter 23). Their trap backfires, and they themselves are trapped by Jesus' question. Three parables follow, the first two of which indirectly answer the question about the source of Jesus' authority.

21:28-32 Saying and doing

The technique Jesus uses is like that of Nathan (2 Sam 12:1-12), whereby the hearers are asked for their opinion and end by pronouncing judgment on themselves. The parable seems a simple one at first. Both children (the word in verse 28 is *teknon*, "child," not *huios*, "son") fall short of the ideal. But the one who appeared to *do* the father's will was the first.

However, in a culture that highly prizes honor, the answer is not so clear. In some manuscript variants of this parable, the one who gives the correct answer is the second child. The first child shamed the father publicly, a worse fault than failing to carry through on one's word. At 7:21-27 Jesus insisted to his disciples that saying *and* doing are necessary; now he directs this message to religious authorities who do not practice what they preach (23:3). Verses 31-32 contrast the leaders, who should most exemplify righteousness, with those who are thought least able to do so. But there is still time for the leaders to repent. Those who initially refuse to say yes to Jesus and do the will of God can still change their minds.

21:33-46 Treacherous tenants

Matthew reworks Mark's version (12:1-12), making the parable more allegorical and more pointedly christological. It is a familiar story, echoing Isaiah 5, but with a new ending. In Isaiah 5 Yahweh decides to destroy the vine-

The Parable of the Two Sons

28"What is your opinion? A man had two sons. He came to the first and said, 'Son, go out and work in the vineyard today.' 29He said in reply, 'I will not,' but afterwards he changed his mind and went. 30The man came to the other son and gave the same order. He said in reply, 'Yes, sir,' but did not go. 31Which of the two did his father's will?" They answered, "The first." Jesus said to them, "Amen, I say to you, tax collectors and prostitutes are entering the kingdom of God before you. 32When John came to you in the way of righteousness, you did not believe him; but tax collectors and prostitutes did. Yet even when you saw that, you did not later change your minds and believe him.

The Parable of the Tenants

33"Hear another parable. There was a landowner who planted a vineyard, put a hedge around it, dug a wine press in it, and built a tower. Then he leased it to tenants and went on a journey. 34When vintage time drew near, he sent his servants to the tenants to obtain his produce. 35But the tenants seized the servants and one they beat, another they killed, and a third they stoned. 36Again he sent other servants, more numerous than the first ones, but they treated them in the same way. 37Finally, he sent his son to them, thinking, 'They will respect my son.' 38But when the

continue

yard after disappointment over the yield of sour grapes from Israel, the carefully cultivated vine. In Jesus' parable the tenants are destroyed; the vineyard remains and is entrusted to others. The eschatological time (*kairos*, v. 34) demands that fruit be evident now (see 21:18-22). The repeated sending of the servants (vv. 34-39) is like God's repeated sending of the prophets to Israel. Prophets were called "servants" of God (Jer 7:25; 25:4; Amos 3:7; Zech 1:6), and their fates match those in the parable (see Jer 20:2; 26:20-23; 2 Chr 24:21).

tenants saw the son, they said to one another, 'This is the heir. Come, let us kill him and acquire his inheritance.' ³⁹They seized him, threw him out of the vineyard, and killed him. ⁴⁰What will the owner of the vineyard do to those tenants when he comes?" ⁴¹They answered him, "He will put those wretched men to a wretched death and lease his vineyard to other tenants who will give him the produce at the proper times." ⁴²Jesus said to them, "Did you never read in the scriptures:

'The stone that the builders rejected
   has become the cornerstone;
by the Lord has this been done,
   and it is wonderful in our eyes'?

⁴³Therefore, I say to you, the kingdom of God will be taken away from you and given to a people that will produce its fruit. ⁴⁴[The one who falls on this stone will be dashed to pieces; and it will crush anyone on whom it falls.]" ⁴⁵When the chief priests and the Pharisees heard his parables, they knew that he was speaking about them. ⁴⁶And although they were attempting to arrest him, they feared the crowds, for they regarded him as a prophet.

continue

The sequence of actions in verse 39 corresponds to the details of Jesus' passion. He is seized (26:50), taken outside the city limits (27:31-32), and then killed (27:35). The murderous plans of the tenants in the vineyard match the intent of the chief priests and Pharisees (21:46; 22:15) toward Jesus. The chief priests and elders pronounce their own self-condemnation (v. 41), but the future tense verbs show that the possibility is yet open so the Jewish leaders can still change their minds (as also 21:29, 32). They could still be among those "other tenants" to whom the vineyard will be entrusted.

Jesus' question in verse 42 (see also 12:3, 5; 19:4; 21:16) underscores the conflict between Jesus' interpretation of Scripture and that of the opposing religious leaders. The quotation from Psalm 118 in verse 42 recalls God's un-

likely choice of David as king, the prototype for the Messiah, and points toward the leadership of the new Israel as coming from those rejected as unimportant. At the conclusion (vv. 45-46) the chief priests and Pharisees clearly understand the parable (cf. 13:51), but instead of heeding Jesus' invitation, they plot his arrest.

22:1-14 Dressed for the feast

This is the third of three parables that Jesus addresses to the religious leaders in Jerusalem after they challenged his authority (21:23-27). The parable is highly allegorized and has a number of unrealistic details. The image of a wedding banquet recalls Matthew 9:15, where Jesus was likened to a groom, whose presence demands feasting, not fasting. This metaphor is frequently used in the Scriptures to signify God's abundant care, both now and at the end time (e.g., Isa 25:6-10; 55:1-3). The repeated invitation is reminiscent of the multiple envoys in 21:33-46 and has an echo of Lady Wisdom inviting all to her banquet (Prov 9:5). The custom of a double invitation (see Esth 5:8; 6:14) allowed the potential guest to find out who the other guests were and whether all was being arranged appropriately. It also gave them time to decide if they would be able to reciprocate. The time lapse also allowed the host to determine the amount of food needed.

Unlike Luke 14:15-24, there are no detailed excuses offered by the invitees. Their mistreatment and killing of the king's servants (vv. 5-6) and the king's enraged response (v. 7), are allegorical allusions to the killing of John the Baptist and the prophets and the destruction of Jerusalem in A.D. 70. The king's retaliation can be expected in an honor-and-shame system, in which one responds in kind to an affront. But his second response (vv. 8-10) is shocking. In a first-century Mediterranean world likes eat with likes, since eating together signifies sharing of values and of social position. The king sends his servants out to the places where the main road cuts through the city boundary, going out to the countryside (v. 10). This is where the poorer people lived, while the elite (5 to 10 percent of the population) lived in the center of the city. Like the parables in 13:24-30, 47-50, both "good" and "bad" are gathered in, and then there is sorting out.

The last scene (vv. 11-14) is entirely unrealistic but highlights Matthew's ethical concern: one must be ready at all times for the end-time banquet, clothed with good deeds (similarly Rom 13:14; Gal 3:27; Col 3:12). More is required of a disciple than initial acceptance of the invitation to be a "friend of God and prophets" (Wis 7:27). See also 20:13, where the grumbler is called "friend," as is Judas at the moment of betrayal (26:50). In the Matthean narrative context, the parable is a warning to the religious leaders who are offered repeated invitations to accept Jesus. The seriousness of their refusal is painted with vivid metaphors: they will be cast into the outer darkness (see also 8:12; 25:30), where there is weeping and gnashing of teeth (8:12, 13:42, 50; 24:51; 25:30). The proverbial saying in verse 14 does not entirely capture the meaning of the parable. The focus is on how those who are expected to respond to the invitation (the religious leaders) refuse, while the unexpected invitees (the socially marginal) have accepted.

22:15-22 Taxes to Caesar

This is the first of four more controversies between Jesus and the religious leaders. Their flattering words (v. 16) are true but insincere, as they proceed to lay a deliberate trap (v. 15). The question is a sticky one. Since the Roman occupation of Palestine in 63 B.C., Jews were obliged to pay tribute, or a head tax, in Roman coinage, on each man, woman, and slave. If Jesus opposes this payment, he would be advocating revolt against Rome. If he advocates payment, then he would be seen as a collaborator with the enemy. Jesus sees the malice and hypocrisy of his questioners, who have set this trap (v. 18). His clever response can be understood in one of three ways: (1) one should pay nothing to Caesar because everything belongs to God (Lev 25:23); (2) one should pay the emperor because he is God's representative (as

---

CHAPTER 22

The Parable of the Wedding Feast

[1]Jesus again in reply spoke to them in parables, saying, [2]"The kingdom of heaven may be likened to a king who gave a wedding feast for his son. [3]He dispatched his servants to summon the invited guests to the feast, but they refused to come. [4]A second time he sent other servants, saying, 'Tell those invited: "Behold, I have prepared my banquet, my calves and fattened cattle are killed, and everything is ready; come to the feast." ' [5]Some ignored the invitation and went away, one to his farm, another to his business. [6]The rest laid hold of his servants, mistreated them, and killed them. [7]The king was enraged and sent his troops, destroyed those murderers, and burned their city. [8]Then he said to his servants, 'The feast is ready, but those who were invited were not worthy to come. [9]Go out, therefore, into the main roads and invite to the feast whomever you find.' [10]The servants went out into the streets and gathered all they found, bad and good alike, and the hall was filled with guests. [11]But when the king came in to meet the guests he saw a man there not dressed in a wedding garment. [12]He said to him, 'My friend, how is it that you came in here without a wedding garment?' But he was reduced to silence. [13]Then the king said to his attendants, 'Bind his hands and feet, and cast him into the darkness outside, where there will be wailing and grinding of teeth.' [14]Many are invited, but few are chosen."

Paying Taxes to the Emperor

[15]Then the Pharisees went off and plotted how they might entrap him in speech. [16]They sent their disciples to him, with the Herodians, saying, "Teacher, we know that you are a truthful man and that you teach the way of God in accordance with the truth. And you are not concerned with anyone's opinion, for you do not regard a person's status. [17]Tell us, then, what is your opinion: Is it lawful to pay the census tax to Caesar or not?" [18]Knowing their malice, Jesus said, "Why are you

continue

testing me, you hypocrites? ¹⁹Show me the coin that pays the census tax." Then they handed him the Roman coin. ²⁰He said to them, "Whose image is this and whose inscription?" ²¹They replied, "Caesar's." At that he said to them, "Then repay to Caesar what belongs to Caesar and to God what belongs to God." ²²When they heard this they were amazed, and leaving him they went away.

The Question about the Resurrection

²³On that day Sadducees approached him, saying that there is no resurrection. They put this question to him, ²⁴saying, "Teacher, Moses said, 'If a man dies without children, his brother shall marry his wife and raise up descendants for his brother.' ²⁵Now there were seven brothers among us. The first married and died and, having no descendants, left his wife to his brother. ²⁶The same happened with the second and the third, through all seven. ²⁷Finally the woman died. ²⁸Now at the resurrection, of the seven, whose wife will she be? For they all had been married to her." ²⁹Jesus said to them in reply, "You are misled because you do not know the scriptures or the power of God. ³⁰At the resurrection they neither marry nor are given in marriage but are like the angels in heaven. ³¹And concerning the resurrection of the dead, have you not read what was said to you by God, ³²'I am the God of Abraham, the God of Isaac, and the God of Jacob'? He is not the God of the dead but of the living." ³³When the crowds heard this, they were astonished at his teaching.

The Greatest Commandment

³⁴When the Pharisees heard that he had silenced the Sadducees, they gathered together, ³⁵and one of them [a scholar of the law] tested him by asking, ³⁶"Teacher, which commandment in the law is the greatest?" ³⁷He said to him, "You shall love the Lord, your God, with all your heart, with all your soul, and with all your mind. ³⁸This is the greatest and the first commandment. ³⁹The second is like it: You shall love your neighbor as

continue

Rom 13:1-7; 1 Pet 2:13-17); (3) one can pay Caesar but recognize that his authority is relative and that loyalty to God takes precedence. The last is the most likely meaning. As in 17:24-27, Jesus advises paying the tax, but this is not a vote of support for the occupying power. The amazed response (v. 22) of the Pharisees' disciples (see also 8:27; 9:33; 15:31; 21:20) underscores Jesus' skill in outwitting his opponents.

22:23-33 The question of resurrection

In this second controversy the Sadducees pose a question that derides belief in the resurrection. Ideas about the afterlife were diverse in Jesus' day. The notion of resurrection of the dead first appears in the book of Daniel (12:2), written in the second century b.c., and was accepted by the Pharisees but not the Sadducees (see Acts 23:6). The situation posed by the Sadducees, citing Deuteronomy 25:5-10, is absurd (although see Tobit 3:8; 6:14, where Sarah, the daughter of Raguel, outlives seven husbands). Like the previous question, it is set up to try to make Jesus contradict his own teaching or the Scriptures. It is a Bible battle in which Jesus emerges as authoritative teacher.

Jesus responds by accusing his opponents of not knowing the Scriptures or the power of God. He cites Exodus 3:6, 15-16 to argue that Israel's ancestors, who were physically dead at the time that God spoke to Moses, continued to be in relationship with God, and so they were in some sense among the living. Jesus also asserts that the Sadducees do not understand the nature of resurrection. By God's power new life will be created that is continuous in some way with the life we have known, yet it will be brought to fullness in ways we do not yet know.

22:34-40 The greatest commandment

In Mark's account (12:28-34; cf. Luke 10:25), the scribe's question is sincere, but in Matthew it leads to another controversy. The Pharisees gather together (v. 34), signaling a plot against Jesus (see 2:4; 22:41; 26:3; 27:17, 27; 28:12; possibly this also alludes to Ps 2:2). The question they pose is meant to test him (see also 22:15).

All commandments are important; all must be kept. The query is not whether some laws can be disregarded, but whether Jesus, like some teachers, would sum up the Torah in a simple statement, as did Rabbi Hillel: "What is hateful to you do not do to your neighbor" (*b. Šabb.* 31a).

Jesus summarizes the whole of the Law in two commandments (see also 7:12). The first, the *Shemaᶜ* (Deut 6:4-9), was recited twice a day by Jews. It enjoins love of God with one's whole heart, soul, and strength. The heart *(kardia)*, was considered the seat of all emotions, the soul *(psychē)*, the center of vitality and consciousness, and strength *(ischys)* denotes power or might. The second command, love of neighbor, is from the Holiness Code (Lev 19:18), which asserts that love of God is manifest in love toward the neighbor. The modern Western notion of the necessity of self-love would have been a foreign concept to people of the biblical world. They did not understand themselves in individualistic terms, but rather as enmeshed in a particular family, clan, and religious group. Dependent on others for their sense of self-identity, love of self and love of others are inseparable.

22:41-46 David's son

In the fourth and final controversy, Jesus is the one who initiates the questioning. Again, the debate centers on the correct interpretation of Scripture. The text in question is Psalm 110:1, a coronation psalm, in which God assures the new king of special honor (sitting at the right hand) and a vanquishing of his enemies (making them subservient, "under your feet"). The speaker in the psalm is David, who says that the "Lord" *(kyrios)*, meaning Yahweh, is speaking to "my lord" *(kyrios)*, meaning the new king.

yourself. [40]The whole law and the prophets depend on these two commandments."

The Question about David's Son

[41]While the Pharisees were gathered together, Jesus questioned them, [42]saying, "What is your opinion about the Messiah? Whose son is he?" They replied, "David's." [43]He said to them, "How, then, does David, inspired by the Spirit, call him 'lord,' saying:

[44]"The Lord said to my lord,
  "Sit at my right hand
    until I place your enemies under your feet"'?

[45]If David calls him 'lord,' how can he be his son?" [46]No one was able to answer him a word, nor from that day on did anyone dare to ask him any more questions.

Jesus stumps his opponents by asking that if David, inspired by the Spirit, calls the new king (here equated with the messiah) "lord," then he must be more than simply his son. The notion that the messiah would be a "son of David" is found in Isaiah 11:1, 10; Jeremiah 23:5. Although this is a favorite Matthean title for Jesus (1:1; 9:27; 12:23; 15:22; 20:30, 31; 21:9, 15), "Son of David" is not adequate to express all that Jesus is. This text brings together several important christological titles intimating that Jesus is also Messiah, Son of God, and Lord. The silence of Jesus' opponents indicates a victory for him. There will be no further exchanges with the leaders until the passion narrative, as he speaks now only with the crowds and his disciples.

EXPLORING LESSON TWO

1. What are some of the messages found in the parable of the workers in the vineyard (20:1-16)? What does it tell us about the kingdom of God?

_____

_____

_____

_____

_____

2. How does Matthew edit Mark's account of the request of James and John to sit at the right and left hand of Jesus in his kingdom (Mark 10:35-45; Matt 20:20-28)? Why does Matthew do so?

_____

_____

_____

_____

_____

3. Jesus says that "the Son of Man did not come to be served but to serve and to give his life as a ransom for many" (20:28). How does the commentary explain the use of the word "many"?

_____

_____

_____

_____

_____

4. What does the final healing story of Matthew's Gospel (20:29-34) teach us about Jesus and about discipleship?

_____

_____

_____

_____

_____

5. How does Matthew draw a contrast between the people's reactions and those of the religious leaders as Jesus enters Jerusalem and cleanses the Temple (21:1-17)?

_____

_____

_____

_____

_____

6. If Jesus were to visit your parish or home, are there any "tables" he might overturn (21:12-13)?

_____

_____

_____

_____

7. How do you interpret Jesus' words to his disciples: "Whatever you ask for in prayer with faith, you will receive"? Is prayer a complicated mystery or a simple act? What does it mean to have "faith"?

_____

_____

_____

_____

_____

8. a) Describe several of the messages that emerge from the three parables that Jesus tells to the religious leaders (21:28-32; 21:33-46; 22:1-14)?

_____

_____

_____

_____

  b) What does Matthew tell us about the religious leaders' response (21:45-46)?

_____

_____

_____

_____

9. The remainder of Matthew 22 includes four debates between Jesus and either the Pharisees or the Sadducees (22:15-22, 23-33, 34-40, 41-46). Choose one of these confrontations and share something that you learned from the commentary or from reflecting on Jesus' words.

_____

_____

_____

_____

_____

_____

_____

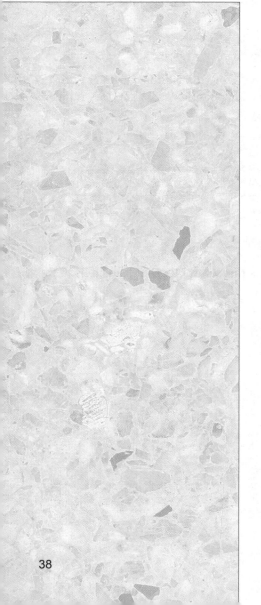

CLOSING PRAYER

Prayer

Jesus stopped and called them and said, "What do you want me to do for you?" They answered him, "Lord, let our eyes be opened." (Matt 20:32-33)

Jesus Christ, Son of David, have pity on us. Open our eyes. Keep us close to you so we may see every act of your compassion, hear every word of your truth, and speak our own *hosannas* in your presence. Open our eyes, our minds, and our hearts as we follow you to Jerusalem. We bring to you in prayer those who are most in need of your healing and compassion, especially . . .

LESSON THREE

Matthew 23–25

Begin your personal study and group discussion with a simple and sincere prayer such as:

Prayer

Loving God, as we read and study your living word, send us the Spirit of Christ, that we may faithfully heed his words and imitate his life.

Read the Bible text of Matthew 23–25 found in the outside columns of pages 40–49, highlighting what stands out to you.

Read the accompanying commentary to add to your understanding.

Respond to the questions on pages 50–53, Exploring Lesson Three.

The Closing Prayer on page 53 is for your personal use and may be used at the end of group discussion.

CHAPTER 23

Denunciation of the Scribes and Pharisees

¹Then Jesus spoke to the crowds and to his disciples, ²saying, "The scribes and the Pharisees have taken their seat on the chair of Moses. ³Therefore, do and observe all things whatsoever they tell you, but do not follow their example. For they preach but they do not practice. ⁴They tie up heavy burdens [hard to carry] and lay them on people's shoulders, but they will not lift a finger to move them. ⁵All their works are performed to be seen. They widen their phylacteries and lengthen their tassels. ⁶They love places of honor at banquets, seats of honor in synagogues, ⁷greetings in marketplaces, and the salutation 'Rabbi.' ⁸As for you, do not be called 'Rabbi.' You have but one teacher, and you are all brothers. ⁹Call no one on earth your father; you have but one Father in heaven. ¹⁰Do not be called 'Master'; you have but one master, the Messiah. ¹¹The greatest among you must be your servant. ¹²Whoever exalts himself will be humbled; but whoever humbles himself will be exalted.

continue

23:1-12 Warning against hypocrisy

The whole of this chapter is a stinging denunciation by Jesus of the scribes and Pharisees, who have been cast as his opponents throughout the Gospel. Matthew expands a brief critique of scribes from Mark 12:38-40, weaving in material from Q and Luke 11:37-52. In the New Testament, scribes are religious leaders who are learned in Torah. Pharisees, lay religious leaders, differed from Sadducees in their belief in resurrection (see 22:23-33) and in oral interpretation of the Law. The excoriating tone of Jesus' rebuke reflects the vehemence of the conflict between the Christians of Matthew's community, who were predominantly Jewish, and the Jews of emerging rabbinic Judaism.

Jesus takes on the role of a prophet, much like Amos (5:18-20; 6:1-7) or Isaiah (5:8-10, 11-14), who uses the classic "woe" form to denounce the wrongdoing of a group of his own people, with the intent to turn them from evil and toward right relation with God. Jesus' words are a warning to the crowds and his disciples (v. 1) not to follow the hypocritical practices of these leaders, who do not practice what they teach (v. 3). In contrast to Jesus, whose burden is light (11:30), they lay heavy loads on people's shoulders (v. 4). They make their phylacteries and fringes noticeable to all (v. 5). (Phylacteries are leather boxes containing the parchment texts such as Exodus 13:1-16; Deuteronomy 6:4-9; 11:13-22, which are strapped to the forehead and arm during morning prayer.) Wearing "tassels" or "fringes" at the corners of the outer garments reminds a Jew to observe all God's commands (Num 15:38-39; Deut 22:12; Matt 9:20; 14:36). Jesus also criticizes the leaders' love of places of honor and deferential titles (vv. 6-10)—only he and God are to bear these titles. Like many other reform movements, there was an impulse in early Christianity toward egalitarianism and status reversal (vv. 11-12; see also 18:1-4; 19:13-15; 20:20-28).

23:13-36 Seven woes

In the seven woes that ensue, the religious leaders are repeatedly called "hypocrites"—a term that originally referred to an actor, one who put on a mask to assume another personage. In the first woe (vv. 13-14), Jesus denounces the scribes and Pharisees not only because they fail to enter into God's realm themselves but, worse yet, they block the way for others. The image of unlocking and locking the way to heaven recalls Matthew 16:19, where Peter is given the keys to God's realm. For Matthew's community, Peter and the leaders of the emergent Christian community are the authorities to be heeded rather than those of the synagogue.

 The designation **"hypocrite"** stems from ancient Greek theater in which players wore masks that portrayed an emotion or attitude illustrative of characters in the play. The root notion, then, is to mask something that covers the true reality. Matthew uses this term frequently with regard to the enemies of Jesus, emphasizing their falsehood (cf. 6:2; 23:15, 23, 25, 27, 29).

The second woe (v. 15) is an accusation that the Gentile converts to Pharisaism are twice as zealous and twice as misguided as their teachers. Jesus warns that in the end they will be "child[ren] of Gehenna" rather than "children of God" (e.g., Matt 5:9, cf. 45). The name "Gehenna" derives from "The Valley (*gē*) of Hinnom," which runs south-southwest of Jerusalem. It represented the place of fiery judgment, because it was there that fires of the cult of Molech and later, smoldering refuse, were located.

In the third woe (vv. 16-22), Jesus critiques the meaningless distinctions the Pharisees invented in their oath-taking. In Jesus' world, binding obligations were set not by contracts but with one's word, by public swearing. For the most serious agreements, God's name would be invoked. But devout Jews objected to speaking God's name aloud. Just as Matthew substituted "the reign of heaven" for "the reign of God" (see 3:2), so Pharisees would

---

13"Woe to you, scribes and Pharisees, you hypocrites. You lock the kingdom of heaven before human beings. You do not enter yourselves, nor do you allow entrance to those trying to enter. [14]

15"Woe to you, scribes and Pharisees, you hypocrites. You traverse sea and land to make one convert, and when that happens you make him a child of Gehenna twice as much as yourselves.

16"Woe to you, blind guides, who say, 'If one swears by the temple, it means nothing, but if one swears by the gold of the temple, one is obligated.' 17Blind fools, which is greater, the gold, or the temple that made the gold sacred? 18And you say, 'If one swears by the altar, it means nothing, but if one swears by the gift on the altar, one is obligated.' 19You blind ones, which is greater, the gift, or the altar that makes the gift sacred? 20One who swears by the altar swears by it and all that is upon it; 21one who swears by the temple swears by it and by him who dwells in it; 22one who swears by heaven swears by the throne of God and by him who is seated on it.

23"Woe to you, scribes and Pharisees, you hypocrites. You pay tithes of mint and dill and cummin, and have neglected the weightier things of the law: judgment and mercy and fidelity. [But] these you should have done, without neglecting the others. 24Blind guides, who strain out the gnat and swallow the camel!

25"Woe to you, scribes and Pharisees, you hypocrites. You cleanse the outside of cup and dish, but inside they are full of plunder and self-indulgence. 26Blind Pharisee, cleanse first the inside of the cup, so that the outside also may be clean.

continue

---

swear on the gold or the gifts of the temple, objects associated with God, as a way to avoid saying the divine name. Jesus says that these fine distinctions are useless; the effect is the same. See Matthew 5:33-37 on not taking oaths at all.

27"Woe to you, scribes and Pharisees, you hypocrites. You are like whitewashed tombs, which appear beautiful on the outside, but inside are full of dead men's bones and every kind of filth. 28Even so, on the outside you appear righteous, but inside you are filled with hypocrisy and evildoing.

29"Woe to you, scribes and Pharisees, you hypocrites. You build the tombs of the prophets and adorn the memorials of the righteous, 30and you say, 'If we had lived in the days of our ancestors, we would not have joined them in shedding the prophets' blood.' 31Thus you bear witness against yourselves that you are the children of those who murdered the prophets; 32now fill up what your ancestors measured out! 33You serpents, you brood of vipers, how can you flee from the judgment of Gehenna? 34Therefore, behold, I send to you prophets and wise men and scribes; some of them you will kill and crucify, some of them you will scourge in your synagogues and pursue from town to town, 35so that there may come upon you all the righteous blood shed upon earth, from the righteous blood of Abel to the blood of Zechariah, the son of Barachiah, whom you murdered between the sanctuary and the altar. 36Amen, I say to you, all these things will come upon this generation.

continue

In the fourth woe (vv. 23-24), Jesus accuses the leaders of not being able to distinguish between what is important and what is not. The texts on tithing (see Lev 27:30-33; Num 18:21-32; Deut 14:22-29) prescribe giving one-tenth of one's produce, flocks, wine, grain, and oil to support the temple, the Levites, and the poor. They do not mention herbs, such as mint, dill, and cumin. Jesus teaches his disciples that their observance of the Law must go beyond what is written (Matt 5:21-48), but the point is to arrive at more complete harmony with God and all that God has created (5:20, 48). The Pharisees, by contrast, engage in intensified practices of keeping the Law that lead them away from deeds of justice, mercy, and faith. Thus they become "blind guides," not seeing the way clearly themselves and leading others onto a destructive path. The outrageousness of their practice is captured in the hyperbole "swallow the camel."

The fifth woe (vv. 25-26) contrasts outer practices with inner dispositions. Jesus uses a strong term, *harpagēs*, "pillage, plunder," to speak of the corrupt inner state of the scribes and Pharisees, who misuse their power to exploit others. He also accuses them of *akrasia*, "lack of self-control" and "want of power" (see v. 25). The reference is to sexual activity or intemperance in general. By contrast, the interior disposition Jesus has taught his disciples is purity of heart (5:8), the ability to forgive from the heart (18:35), and love of God with all one's heart (22:37).

The sixth woe (vv. 27-28) continues in the same vein as the fifth. The Pharisees and scribes present a lovely exterior, seeming to be in right relation with God and others, while their interior disposition is rotten with hypocrisy and evildoing. Like white-washed sepulchers, they hide putrid decay within. White-washing sepulchers made them easily visible, so that Jews could avoid contact with them and thus maintain ritual purity (see Lev 21:1, 11).

In the seventh and last woe (vv. 29-36), the Pharisees and scribes pretend to honor the prophets and righteous ancestors with decorated monuments and protest that had they been alive earlier, they would never have done what their ancestors did to the prophets. In truth, Jesus says, they are no different from their forebears. They will kill the prophet Jesus just as their ancestors rid themselves of the pesky prophets who denounced their unrighteousness. They show themselves to be not children of God but children of Gehenna (v. 15) and children of murderers (v. 31), linked to all the innocent blood shed from Abel to Zechariah, the first victim of murder in the Bible (Gen 4:8) to the last. There is some confusion about the identity of Zechariah. The Old Testament prophet Zechariah was the son of Barachiah (Zech 1:1), but as far as we know, he was not murdered "between the sanctuary and the altar" (v. 35), as was Zechariah, son of Jehoiada (2 Chr 24:20-22).

The theme of responsibility for innocent blood is an important one in the passion narrative as Judas tries to return the blood money (27:4), Pilate tries to wash himself of guilt for Jesus' blood (27:24), and the people say to Pilate, "His blood be on us and on our children" (27:25). At the Last Supper Jesus offers to his disciples his "blood of the covenant" (26:28) for the forgiveness of sins.

23:37-39 Lament over Jerusalem

The tone shifts from vehement denunciation of the leaders to profound sadness for the city which destroys God's messengers and which, by Matthew's day, lies in ruins. The poignant image of a mother bird yearning to gather her rebellious young under her wings is a common metaphor in the Scriptures for God's loving care (Deut 32:11; Ruth 2:12; Pss 17:8; 36:7; 57:1; 61:4; Luke 13:34-35). But like a mother who never abandons even the most wayward child, Jesus, quoting Psalm 118:26, holds out the promise that they will see him again when they can receive him as did the disciples when he first entered Jerusalem (21:9).

The denunciations and woes in this chapter must always be read in the context of a bitter internal family dispute between the Jewish Christians and Jews who did not join them in Matthew's day. Jesus is a prophet admonishing his own leaders and inviting them to a change of heart. His words still sound a warning against hypocrisy to any religious leaders.

24:1–25:46 The apocalyptic discourse

Jesus has been teaching his disciples and warning and disputing with other religious leaders since 21:23. He now leaves the temple area and directs his instruction only to his disciples (24:1, 3). He speaks of the calamities that presage the coming of the Human One (24:1-33) and tells three parables (24:45–25:30) that emphasize the need for watchfulness. The parable of the final judgment (25:31-46) brings this last block of teaching to a climax.

The Lament over Jerusalem

[37]"Jerusalem, Jerusalem, you who kill the prophets and stone those sent to you, how many times I yearned to gather your children together, as a hen gathers her young under her wings, but you were unwilling! [38]Behold, your house will be abandoned, desolate. [39]I tell you, you will not see me again until you say, 'Blessed is he who comes in the name of the Lord.'"

CHAPTER 24

The Destruction of the Temple Foretold

[1]Jesus left the temple area and was going away, when his disciples approached him to point out the temple buildings. [2]He said to them in reply, "You see all these things, do you not? Amen, I say to you, there will not be left here a stone upon another stone that will not be thrown down."

The Beginning of Calamities

[3]As he was sitting on the Mount of Olives, the disciples approached him privately and said, "Tell us, when will this happen, and what sign will there be of your coming, and of the end of the age?" [4]Jesus said to them in reply, "See that no one

continue

24:1-14 The beginning of the end

The tension between Jesus and the temple leadership has been mounting. He has performed a prophetic action of purification in the temple (21:12-17), he has engaged in debates with the temple leadership (21:23–22:46), and he has warned his disciples about their hypocrisy (23:1-36). This comes to a head as Jesus now predicts the very destruction of the temple (24:1-2), an occurrence that Jeremiah (7:1-15) associated with the messianic age. In Matthew's day this has already occurred. At his interrogation before the Jewish leaders, false witnesses accuse Jesus of making threats against the temple (26:61) and passersby deride him about this in the crucifixion scene (27:40).

deceives you. [5]For many will come in my name, saying, 'I am the Messiah,' and they will deceive many. [6]You will hear of wars and reports of wars; see that you are not alarmed, for these things must happen, but it will not yet be the end. [7]Nation will rise against nation, and kingdom against kingdom; there will be famines and earthquakes from place to place. [8]All these are the beginning of the labor pains. [9]Then they will hand you over to persecution, and they will kill you. You will be hated by all nations because of my name. [10]And then many will be led into sin; they will betray and hate one another. [11]Many false prophets will arise and deceive many; [12]and because of the increase of evildoing, the love of many will grow cold. [13]But the one who perseveres to the end will be saved. [14]And this gospel of the kingdom will be preached throughout the world as a witness to all nations, and then the end will come.

The Great Tribulation

[15]"When you see the desolating abomination spoken of through Daniel the prophet standing in the holy place (let the reader understand), [16]then in Judea must flee to the mountains, [17]a person on the housetop must not go down to get things out of his house, [18]a person in the field must not return to get his cloak. [19]Woe to pregnant women and nursing mothers in those days. [20]Pray that your flight not be in winter or on the sabbath, [21]for at that time there will be great tribulation, such as has not been since the beginning of the world until now, nor ever will be. [22]And if those days had not been shortened, no one would be saved; but for the sake of the elect they will be shortened. [23]If anyone says to you then, 'Look, here is the Messiah!' or, 'There he is!' do not believe it. [24]False messiahs and false prophets will arise, and they will perform signs and wonders so great as to deceive, if that were possible, even the elect. [25]Behold, I have told it to you beforehand. [26]So if they say to you, 'He is in the desert,' do not go out there; if they say, 'He is in the inner rooms,' do not believe it. [27]For just as

continue

Jesus then speaks about the signs of the end times. He is seated, as authoritative teacher (see also 5:10; 15:29), on the Mount of Olives, the place associated with the final judgment (Zech 14:4). As in the parable discourse (13:10-17), Jesus' disciples receive private instruction. He paints a picture of massive chaos and destruction, with a proliferation of false messiahs, wars, famines, earthquakes, persecution, hatred because of Jesus' name, sin, betrayal, deception, lawlessness, and loss of fervor. Strife comes both from within and from without.

In almost every age people see these signs and wonder if they herald the end. A similar theme is found in the mission discourse (10:16-25, 34-39), where Jesus also assured his disciples not to fear anything because of God's constant care for them (10:26-33). Here as well, Jesus tells them that if they persevere to the end, they will be saved (v. 13). These birth pangs (v. 8) are the prelude to new life. For Matthew, this end is not imminent—the Gospel must first be preached throughout the whole world (see also 28:16-20).

24:15-31 Signs of the coming of the Human One

There will be unmistakable signs when the end actually does come. It will be as evident as lightning across the sky (v. 27) or vultures circling over a corpse (v. 28). One sign will be like the one spoken of by Daniel, the "desolating abomination" (v. 15; Dan 9:27; 11:31; 12:11). In Daniel this referred to the statue that Antiochus IV Epiphanes placed in the temple in 167 B.C., which sparked the Maccabean revolt. Still fresh in the memories of Matthew's community is that the emperor Caligula threatened a similar action in A.D. 40.

A future event of this caliber will signal the end. This is a time when immediate flight is the response to the danger (as in 2:12-13, 10:23). As is so often the case, it is mothers and children who are the most adversely affected. The disciples are to pray that it not happen at a time when the hardship would be intensified, such as winter or the sabbath. Fleeing on the sabbath

(v. 20) may have drawn attention to the community and put them at risk. Or it could be a cause of division if some thought flight would break sabbath observance.

Cosmic signs (as in Isa 13:10; 34:4; Ezek 32:7; Joel 2:10, 31; 3:4; 4:15; Amos 8:9; Hag 2:6, 21) preface the final sign before the coming of the Son of Man/the Human One. Why mourning (v. 30) will accompany this sign is not clear—is it because of the tribulations or because people are repenting? The motif of God gathering in the elect at the end time is a common one (Deut 30:3-4; Isa 11:11-12; Ezek 37:21; 39:27-29; Zech 2:6-12).

24:32-51 Parables of watchfulness

A series of parables and figurative sayings exhorts disciples to watchfulness. The fig tree (vv. 32-35), which is different from other trees in Palestine (most are evergreens), sheds all its leaves in winter. Just as its budding is a sign of the arrival of summer, the signs in the previous verses alert disciples to the coming of the Human One. There is a tension between verse 34, which assures that the end is imminent, and verse 14, which asserts that the Gospel first has to be preached to the whole world. Disciples need to be both ready and steadfast, trusting in Jesus' words, which will never pass away (similarly the Torah, 5:18). The timing of the end is unpredictable, so disciples need to stay awake (see also 26:38, 40, 41).

While the previous verses emphasize watchfulness for the coming of the master, the parable of the faithful servant (vv. 45-51) exhorts disciples to vigilance in day-to-day tasks that must be fulfilled in the in-between time. One of these is the daily distribution of food (v. 45). This detail may be an allusion to the difficulties in the early church over food and eating, such as conflicts over Gentile and Jewish Christians eating together (Gal 2:11-14) or having people of differing social status at the same table (22:1-14). Alternatively, giving food may be understood as a metaphor for teaching (see 1 Cor 3:2; John 6:25-33), and the parable as an exhortation to leaders to exercise their

lightning comes from the east and is seen as far as the west, so will the coming of the Son of Man be. [28]Wherever the corpse is, there the vultures will gather.

The Coming of the Son of Man

[29]"Immediately after the tribulation of those days,

the sun will be darkened,
and the moon will not give its light,
and the stars will fall from the sky,
and the powers of the heavens will be shaken.

[30]And then the sign of the Son of Man will appear in heaven, and all the tribes of the earth will mourn, and they will see the Son of Man coming upon the clouds of heaven with power and great glory. [31]And he will send out his angels with a trumpet blast, and they will gather his elect from the four winds, from one end of the heavens to the other.

The Lesson of the Fig Tree

[32]"Learn a lesson from the fig tree. When its branch becomes tender and sprouts leaves, you know that summer is near. [33]In the same way, when you see all these things, know that he is near, at the gates. [34]Amen, I say to you, this generation will not pass away until all these things have taken place. [35]Heaven and earth will pass away, but my words will not pass away.

The Unknown Day and Hour

[36]"But of that day and hour no one knows, neither the angels of heaven, nor the Son, but the Father alone. [37]For as it was in the days of Noah, so it will be at the coming of the Son of Man. [38]In [those] days before the flood, they were eating and drinking, marrying and giving in marriage, up to the day that Noah entered the ark. [39]They did not know until the flood came and carried them all away. So will it be [also] at the coming of the Son of Man. [40]Two men will be out in the field; one

continue

will be taken, and one will be left. [41]Two women will be grinding at the mill; one will be taken, and one will be left. [42]Therefore, stay awake! For you do not know on which day your Lord will come. [43]Be sure of this: if the master of the house had known the hour of night when the thief was coming, he would have stayed awake and not let his house be broken into. [44]So too, you also must be prepared, for at an hour you do not expect, the Son of Man will come.

The Faithful or the Unfaithful Servant

[45]"Who, then, is the faithful and prudent servant, whom the master has put in charge of his household to distribute to them their food at the proper time? [46]Blessed is that servant whom his master on his arrival finds doing so. [47]Amen, I say to you, he will put him in charge of all his property. [48]But if that wicked servant says to himself, 'My master is long delayed,' [49]and begins to beat his fellow servants, and eat and drink with drunkards, [50]the servant's master will come on an unexpected day and at an unknown hour [51]and will punish him severely and assign him a place with the hypocrites, where there will be wailing and grinding of teeth.

CHAPTER 25

The Parable of the Ten Virgins

[1]"Then the kingdom of heaven will be like ten virgins who took their lamps and went out to meet the bridegroom. [2]Five of them were foolish and five were wise. [3]The foolish ones, when taking their lamps, brought no oil with them, [4]but the wise brought flasks of oil with their lamps. [5]Since the bridegroom was long delayed, they all became drowsy and fell asleep. [6]At midnight, there was a cry, 'Behold, the bridegroom! Come out to meet him!' [7]Then all those virgins got up and trimmed their lamps. [8]The foolish ones said to the wise, 'Give us some of your oil, for our lamps are going out.' [9]But the wise ones replied, 'No, for there may not be enough for us and you. Go instead to the

continue

teaching ministry well. The warning to those who gorge themselves on the resources meant for the community is dire; such a one will be dismembered (*dichotomēsei*, literally, "cut in two," v. 51) as a condemned person.

25:1-13 Ready maidens

A second parable advising preparedness for the coming of the Human One casts Jesus in the role of a bridegroom (as 9:15; see Isa 54:5; Jer 31:32; Hos 2:16, where Yahweh is the bridegroom of Israel). In Jesus' day, weddings took place in two stages. First was the betrothal ceremony at the home of the father of the bride, at which the groom presented the marriage contract and the bride price to his future father-in-law. The bride continued to live in her father's house until the second step, when she would move to the home of her husband, about a year later. This is the stage depicted in the parable. The maidens are waiting while the groom and the bride's father hammer out the final negotiations. Upon reaching a final agreement, the wedding party would go in procession to the house of the groom, where the feasting would commence.

The waiting women are friends of the groom; the bride is never mentioned in the story. The word *parthenos* refers to a virgin, a young woman of marriageable age (twelve or in her early teens). The contrast between wise and foolish recalls the builders in 7:24-27. It is not clear whether the women are carrying torches (the usual connotation of *lampades*) wrapped with oil-soaked rags or handheld oil lamps with lighted wicks. Matthew 5:14-16 provides a clue to interpreting why the women cannot share their oil. There light is equated with good deeds that are visible to others and lead to praise of God. Similarly, at Matthew 7:24-27 the wise are those who hear and act on Jesus' words. Just so, the wise maidens in this parable are those who have faithfully prepared for the end time. No one can supply this preparation for another. One is either ready or not at the eschatological moment.

25:14-30 Investing talents

This parable is often interpreted as an exhortation to use all one's God-given gifts to the full. However, the Greek word *talanton* has no other connotation than a monetary unit or weight measurement. In the parable it denotes a very large sum of money. What the parable depicts are two servants who invest and double the money with which they are entrusted, which wins them their master's approval, a share in his joy, and further responsibility. The third servant, by contrast, buries the money, which was considered the best way of safeguarding valuables in antiquity. Yet he earns harsh punishment from the master.

Key to understanding the parable is that Jesus did not live in a capitalist system, where it was thought that wealth can be increased by investment. Rather, people had a notion of limited good: there is only so much wealth, and any increase to one person takes away from another. The aim in life for a peasant was to have enough to take care of his family. Anyone amassing large amounts for himself would be seen as greedy and wicked. In the parable, then, if the master is not a figure for God, it is the third servant who is the honorable one—only he has refused to collaborate with his master in his unfettered greed. The parable warns rich people to stop exploiting those who are poor, and it encourages poor people to take courageous measures to expose greed for the sin that it is. The last verse is sobering, depicting what can happen to those who oppose the rich and powerful. It can encourage disciples to find ways to stand together as they confront unjust systems. There is still opportunity, since the end time has not yet arrived.

25:31-46 Final judgment

This is the last of Matthew's parables and is unique to this Gospel. The time of judgment has arrived as the Human One comes in his glory (v. 31). This scene is intimately linked with 28:16-20, where Jesus instructs his followers to make disciples of all nations (*panta ta ethnē*, 28:19), a command that this parable presumes has been fulfilled. All the nations (v. 32)

merchants and buy some for yourselves.' [10]While they went off to buy it, the bridegroom came and those who were ready went into the wedding feast with him. Then the door was locked. [11]Afterwards the other virgins came and said, 'Lord, Lord, open the door for us!' [12]But he said in reply, 'Amen, I say to you, I do not know you.' [13]Therefore, stay awake, for you know neither the day nor the hour.

The Parable of the Talents

[14]"It will be as when a man who was going on a journey called in his servants and entrusted his possessions to them. [15]To one he gave five talents; to another, two; to a third, one—to each according to his ability. Then he went away. Immediately [16]the one who received five talents went and traded with them, and made another five. [17]Likewise, the one who received two made another two. [18]But the man who received one went off and dug a hole in the ground and buried his master's money. [19]After a long time the master of those servants came back and settled accounts with them. [20]The one who had received five talents came forward bringing the additional five. He said, 'Master, you gave me five talents. See, I have made five more.' [21]His master said to him, 'Well done, my good and faithful servant. Since you were faithful in small matters, I will give you great responsibilities. Come, share your master's joy.' [22][Then] the one who had received two talents also came forward and said, 'Master, you gave me two talents. See, I have made two more.' [23]His master said to him, 'Well done, my good and faithful servant. Since you were faithful in small matters, I will give you great responsibilities. Come, share your master's joy.' [24]Then the one who had received the one talent came forward and said, 'Master, I knew you were a demanding person, harvesting where you did not plant and gathering where you did not scatter; [25]so out of fear I went off and buried your talent in the ground. Here it is back.' [26]His master said to him in reply, 'You wicked, lazy servant! So you knew that I harvest where I did not plant and gather

continue

where I did not scatter? [27]Should you not then have put my money in the bank so that I could have got it back with interest on my return? [28]Now then! Take the talent from him and give it to the one with ten. [29]For to everyone who has, more will be given and he will grow rich; but from the one who has not, even what he has will be taken away. [30]And throw this useless servant into the darkness outside, where there will be wailing and grinding of teeth.'

The Judgment of the Nations

[31]"When the Son of Man comes in his glory, and all the angels with him, he will sit upon his glorious throne, [32]and all the nations will be assembled before him. And he will separate them one from another, as a shepherd separates the sheep from the goats. [33]He will place the sheep on his right and the goats on his left. [34]Then the king will say to those on his right, 'Come, you who are blessed by my Father. Inherit the kingdom prepared for you from the foundation of the world. [35]For I was hungry and you gave me food, I was thirsty and you gave me drink, a stranger and you welcomed me, [36]naked and you clothed me, ill and you cared for me, in prison and you visited me.' [37]Then the righteous will answer him and say, 'Lord, when did we see you hungry and feed you, or thirsty and give you drink? [38]When did we see you a stranger and welcome you, or naked and clothe you? [39]When did we see you ill or in prison, and visit you?' [40]And the king will say to them in reply, 'Amen, I say to you, whatever you did for one of these least brothers of mine, you did for me.' [41]Then he will say to those on his left, 'Depart from me, you accursed, into the eternal fire prepared for the devil and his angels. [42]For I was hungry and you gave me no food, I was thirsty and you gave me no drink, [43]a stranger and you gave me no welcome, naked and you gave me no clothing, ill and in prison, and you did not care for me.' [44]Then they will answer and say, 'Lord, when did we see you hungry or thirsty or a stranger or naked or ill or in prison, and not

continue

are now assembled to render account. The reason why the sheep are separated from the goats is not clear. Both were very valuable. Nor is there any evidence that after pasturing them together during the daytime, a shepherd would separate the two at night. (See 3:12; 13:24-30, 47-50; 24:40-41; 25:1-13 for other images of end-time separation.) Since most people were right-handed and developed greater strength and skill with this hand, the right side came to symbolize favor, blessing, and honor.

 Matthew's famous judgment scene of the sheep and goats evokes the church's tradition of the **corporal works of mercy.** For Jesus there is an intimate connection between love of God and love of neighbor (Matthew 22:37-40). One cannot profess to love God and then not respond to the needs of other human beings. In church tradition the corporal works of mercy are concrete actions that put love of God into practice: "feeding the hungry, sheltering the homeless, clothing the naked, visiting the sick and imprisoned, and burying the dead" (*Catechism of the Catholic Church*, 2447).

The image of Jesus shifts from shepherd to king (v. 34; see 2:2; 21:5). And, like Moses, who laid out before the Israelites the choice of blessing or curse (Deut 11:26), Jesus separates those "blessed by my Father" (v. 34) from those "accursed" (v. 41). This is not predestined; rather, God's invitation goes out to all (5:45; 13:3-9), and the choice to accept or reject it rests with each. For those who accept the invitation, which is visible in their deeds, blessing and inheritance in God's realm await.

In light of the saying at 24:14, it is likely that Matthew envisions the completion of the great commission (28:16-20); all people, including Israel, Gentiles, and Christians, have heard the Gospel and are now judged according to their deeds. The "least brothers" (v. 40) and "least ones" (v. 45) most likely refer to other Christians rather than to just any person in need. See

11:11; 18:6, 14, where "little ones" and "least" refer to vulnerable members of the Christian community, and 10:41-42, where Jesus promises the reward of a righteous person for those who receive the needy ones sent out on mission. The basis of judgment, then, is how one receives Jesus through his followers who proclaim the Gospel (see 10:40).

minister to your needs?' ⁴⁵He will answer them, 'Amen, I say to you, what you did not do for one of these least ones, you did not do for me.' ⁴⁶And these will go off to eternal punishment, but the righteous to eternal life."

EXPLORING LESSON THREE

1. How might we take Jesus' warnings concerning the hypocrisy of the religious leaders of his time and apply them as a warning against hypocrisy in ourselves (23:1-12)?

_____

_____

_____

_____

_____

2. The commentary notes the "excoriating tone" of Jesus' rebukes of the scribes and Pharisees in 23:1-36. Although the words and tone reflect the tense religious situation of Matthew's Jewish-Christian community, the Gospels demonstrate that Jesus did not shy away from confrontation when he felt that it was necessary. What is your experience of reading these strong words of Jesus? Does it make you uncomfortable to think of Jesus overturning tables in the temple and speaking harsh "woes" to religious leaders? Why or why not?

_____

_____

_____

_____

_____

3. Jesus laments over Jerusalem with the yearning of a mother for her children (23:37-39). How does this image add to your understanding of God? (See also Deut 32:11; Ruth 2:12; Ps 61:5; Isa 66:13.)

_____

_____

_____

_____

4. a) What are several of the signs that will precede "the end" (24:1-14)?

_____

_____

_____

_____

b) Does this seem to be something that is going to happen immediately or after some time?

_____

_____

_____

_____

_____

_____

c) What comforting words does Jesus offer his disciples in the midst of these warnings?

_____

_____

_____

_____

_____

_____

5. Jesus warns that "false messiahs and false prophets" will arise before the Son of Man comes and will deceive many people with their "signs and wonders" (24:24). What do you think are some ways that we can discern what is truly of Christ and what is not? (See 1 Thess 5:21.)

_____

_____

_____

_____

_____

6. How does the commentary explain why the wise virgins cannot share their oil (25:1-13; see also Matt 5:14-16)? What does this tell us about the way we live our lives on a daily basis?

_____

_____

_____

_____

_____

_____

7. a) The commentary offers a unique interpretation of the parable of the talents, where the master is not seen as a figure for God. Using this interpretation, what message might we gain from this parable (25:14-30)?

_____

_____

_____

_____

_____

b) This parable is traditionally interpreted in a way that identifies the master with God. If you read the parable with this understanding, what message does it address to you personally?

_____

_____

_____

_____

_____

_____

8. a) Who are the "least" in your community (25:40, 45)?

_____

_____

_____

_____

_____

_____

b) How might the parable of the sheep and the goats encourage outreach and ministry to those who are considered the "least"?

_____

_____

_____

_____

_____

_____

9. How does the message in this parable of the sheep and the goats (25:31-46) exemplify Jesus' earlier teaching concerning the greatest commandment (22:36-40)?

_____

_____

_____

_____

_____

_____

CLOSING PRAYER

Prayer

"Therefore, stay awake! For you do not know on which day your Lord will come."

(Matt 24:42)

Jesus our Teacher, through your teachings and parables you encourage us to live in readiness, faithfulness, and love until you return. As we wait for you with ready hearts, impel us to love you in others by feeding the hungry, visiting the lonely, and caring for the sick among us. May we always be aware of your presence in the least of our brothers and sisters. Today we pray especially for . . .

LESSON FOUR

Matthew 26–28

Begin your personal study and group discussion with a simple and sincere prayer such as:

Prayer

Loving God, as we read and study your living word, send us the Spirit of Christ, that we may faithfully heed his words and imitate his life.

Read the Bible text of Matthew 26–28 found in the outside columns of pages 56–69, highlighting what stands out to you.

Read the accompanying commentary to add to your understanding.

Respond to the questions on pages 70–73, Exploring Lesson Four.

The Closing Prayer on page 73 is for your personal use and may be used at the end of group discussion.

VII: The Passion and Resurrection

CHAPTER 26

The Conspiracy against Jesus

¹When Jesus finished all these words, he said to his disciples, ²"You know that in two days' time it will be Passover, and the Son of Man will be handed over to be crucified." ³Then the chief priests and the elders of the people assembled in the palace of the high priest, who was called Caiaphas, ⁴and they consulted together to arrest Jesus by treachery and put him to death. ⁵But they said, "Not during the festival, that there may not be a riot among the people."

The Anointing at Bethany

⁶Now when Jesus was in Bethany in the house of Simon the leper, ⁷a woman came up to him with an alabaster jar of costly perfumed oil, and poured it on his head while he was reclining at table. ⁸When the disciples saw this, they were indignant and said, "Why this waste? ⁹It could have been sold for much, and the money given to the poor." ¹⁰Since Jesus knew this, he said to them, "Why do you make trouble for the woman? She has done a good thing for me. ¹¹The poor you will always have with you; but you will not always have me. ¹²In pouring this perfumed oil upon my body, she did it to prepare me for burial. ¹³Amen, I say to you, wherever this gospel is proclaimed in the whole world, what she has done will be spoken of, in memory of her."

The Betrayal by Judas

¹⁴Then one of the Twelve, who was called Judas Iscariot, went to the chief priests ¹⁵and said, "What are you willing to give me if I hand him over to you?" They paid him thirty pieces of silver, ¹⁶and from that time on he looked for an opportunity to hand him over.

Preparations for the Passover

¹⁷On the first day of the Feast of Unleavened Bread, the disciples approached Jesus and said,

continue

26:1–27:66 The passion and resurrection

Matthew's usual formula at the end of a block of teaching, "When Jesus finished . . ." (26:1, as also 7:28; 11:1; 13:53; 19:1), marks the transition to the passion narrative. There is also an echo of Deuteronomy 32:45, where Moses finished his instruction to Israel and then prepared for his death. In these final scenes Matthew follows Mark closely, while adding his own unique touches. Jesus is portrayed as knowing what will happen and as being in control of the events. As Matthew is wont to do, he interprets each action as fulfilling the Scriptures.

26:1-16 Preparation for death: Treacherous plotting and prophetic anointing

For the fourth and last time (16:21; 17:22-23; 20:18-19), Jesus predicts his death. The prime movers are the chief priests and elders (v. 3), along with the high priest, Caiaphas (v. 3), who held office from A.D. 18 to 36. The Pharisees and scribes, who have been Jesus' opponents up to this point in the narrative, drop out of view until 27:62. The people are still basically favorable toward Jesus (v. 5).

In strong contrast to the leaders' treachery is the action of an anonymous woman who anoints Jesus in the home of Simon the leper. This takes place in Bethany, a village just east of Jerusalem, over the Mount of Olives. In the Gospel of John this is identified as the home of Martha, Mary, and Lazarus (John 11:1–12:12). By anointing Jesus' head, the woman takes on the role of priest and prophet. She both prepares Jesus for burial (v. 12) and commissions him as messianic king (see Sam 16:12-13; 1 Kgs 1:39). Jesus affirms her action, over the objection of the disciples. There is no question of a lack of concern for the poor by Jesus (see 5:3, 42; 6:2-4, 24; 19:21; 25:31-46); rather, the issue is the timing and the woman's recognition of Jesus' fate. She embodies the understanding and loyalty of the women disciples who, in contrast to the others (26:56), remain to see the crucifixion (27:55-56), keep vigil at the tomb (27:61), and are the first to encounter the risen Christ (28:1-10). Her pouring of oil on Jesus' head (v. 6) prefigures Jesus' pouring out of his blood for all (v. 28). While her action is remembered (v. 13), her identity is not.

In strong contrast is the act of Judas (vv. 14-16), who negotiates with the chief priests to hand Jesus over to them. No motive is given (cf. John 12:6). Once again Matthew interprets this deed through Scripture. Thirty pieces of silver is the worth of a slave (Exod 21:32). But probably the allusion is to Zechariah 11:12-13, where this is the amount of a shepherd's wage, which Judas casts back into the treasury (see 27:3-10).

26:17-35 The Last Supper

As the woman prepared Jesus for his passion, so now Jesus prepares his disciples. In the first scene (vv. 17-19), the disciples approach (*prosēlthon*, the reverential stance also of the woman in v. 7; also 4:3, 11; 5:1; 8:2) Jesus and ask about Passover preparations. Jesus' reply has an apocalyptic nuance, as Matthew uses both *kairos*, "appointed time" (8:29; cf. 13:30; 16:3; 21:34), and *engiken*, "draws near" (cf. 3:2; 4:17; 10:7; 21:34; 24:32-33) in reference to the end time.

The meal begins with a notation that Jesus is with his disciples (v. 20). His words and actions interpret for his intimate followers ("Twelve" is symbolic for all, as also 10:1-4)

"Where do you want us to prepare for you to eat the Passover?" [18]He said, "Go into the city to a certain man and tell him, 'The teacher says, "My appointed time draws near; in your house I shall celebrate the Passover with my disciples."'" [19]The disciples then did as Jesus had ordered, and prepared the Passover.

The Betrayer

[20]When it was evening, he reclined at table with the Twelve. [21]And while they were eating, he said, "Amen, I say to you, one of you will betray me." [22]Deeply distressed at this, they began to say to him one after another, "Surely it is not I, Lord?" [23]He said in reply, "He who has dipped his hand into the dish with me is the one who will betray me. [24]The Son of Man indeed goes, as it is written of him, but woe to that man by whom the Son of Man is betrayed. It would be better for that man if he had never been born." [25]Then Judas, his betrayer, said in reply, "Surely it is not I, Rabbi?" He answered, "You have said so."

The Lord's Supper

[26]While they were eating, Jesus took bread, said the blessing, broke it, and giving it to his disciples said, "Take and eat; this is my body." [27]Then he took a cup, gave thanks, and gave it to them, saying, "Drink from it, all of you, [28]for this is my blood of the covenant, which will be shed on behalf of many for the forgiveness of sins. [29]I tell you, from now on I shall not drink this fruit of the vine until the day when I drink it with you new in the kingdom of my Father." [30]Then, after singing a hymn, they went out to the Mount of Olives.

Peter's Denial Foretold

[31]Then Jesus said to them, "This night all of you will have your faith in me shaken, for it is written:

'I will strike the shepherd,
   and the sheep of the flock will be
      dispersed';

continue

³²but after I have been raised up, I shall go before you to Galilee." ³³Peter said to him in reply, "Though all may have their faith in you shaken, mine will never be." ³⁴Jesus said to him, "Amen, I say to you, this very night before the cock crows, you will deny me three times." ³⁵Peter said to him, "Even though I should have to die with you, I will not deny you." And all the disciples spoke likewise.

The Agony in the Garden

³⁶Then Jesus came with them to a place called Gethsemane, and he said to his disciples, "Sit here while I go over there and pray." ³⁷He took along Peter and the two sons of Zebedee, and began to feel sorrow and distress. ³⁸Then he said to them, "My soul is sorrowful even to death. Remain here and keep watch with me." ³⁹He advanced a little and fell prostrate in prayer, saying, "My Father, if it is possible, let this cup pass from me; yet, not as I will, but as you will." ⁴⁰When he returned to his disciples he found them asleep. He said to Peter, "So you could not keep watch with me for one hour? ⁴¹Watch and pray that you may not undergo the test. The spirit is willing, but the flesh is weak." ⁴²Withdrawing a second time, he prayed again, "My Father, if it is not possible that this cup pass without my drinking it, your will be done!" ⁴³Then he returned once more and found them asleep, for they could not keep their eyes open. ⁴⁴He left them and withdrew again and prayed a third time, saying the same thing again. ⁴⁵Then he returned to his disciples and said to them, "Are you still sleeping and taking your rest? Behold, the hour is at hand when the Son of Man is to be handed over to sinners. ⁴⁶Get up, let us go. Look, my betrayer is at hand."

continue

tween the obedience of Jesus (v. 24) and the disobedience of Judas, who calls Jesus "Rabbi" (vv. 25 and 49), after Jesus has instructed his disciples not to use that address (23:8). The allusion to Psalm 41:10 in verse 23 captures the anguish of betrayal by an intimate friend. Typically, Matthew signals the dire consequences of not acting justly with a pronunciation of woe (as 11:21; 18:7; 23:13, 15, 16, 23, 25, 27, 29; 24:19). Unique to Matthew is the personal exchange between Judas and Jesus (v. 25; also 26:49-50). Jesus' enigmatic "you have said so" is the same response he gives to the high priest (26:64) and to Pilate (27:11).

The institution of the Eucharist (vv. 26-29) is the core and climax of this section. Jesus' gift of self in the form of bread is reminiscent of the feedings of the multitudes (14:13-21; 15:32-39) and of the similar actions by Elijah and Elisha (1 Kgs 17: 8-16; 2 Kgs 4:42-44), as well as of God's provision of manna in the desert for Israel (Exod 16). The cup in which all participate symbolizes both his death (see 20:22; 26:39, 42) and a ratification of a renewed life in covenantal fidelity. Blood, as the symbol of life (Deut 12:23), was sprinkled by Moses on the altar and on the people (Exod 24:8) to seal the covenant.

A unique element in Matthew's account is the interpretation that this action is "on behalf of many, for the forgiveness of sins" (v. 28). This is an allusion to the servant in Isaiah 53:4-12 (see also 12:17-21; 20:28). The "many" (*pollōn*) is a Semitic expression meaning "all"; no one is excluded from the saving effects of Jesus' death (see 1:21). Forgiveness is possible even for those who hand Jesus over to death. The gift of bread and wine also sounds an eschatological note, as the messianic banquet of Isaiah 25:6-9 is in view. Jesus assures his disciples that while the intimacy of eating and drinking together, which they shared during his earthly life, is ending, they will yet experience this with him in the realm of God (v. 29).

The scene shifts to the Mount of Olives (v. 31; see 24:3), where jubilant singing (Psalms 114–118 are sung at the conclusion of the Passover meal) gives way to a sober prediction by

how he is still present with them ("Emmanuel," 1:23; cf. 28:20), even when his earthly life ends. Tragic predictions of betrayal (vv. 20-25) and denial (vv. 31-35) by his closest disciples frame Jesus' eucharistic words and actions (vv. 26-30). In verses 20-25 there is a contrast be-

Jesus that all the disciples will have their faith shaken (*skandalizesthai*, literally, to find Jesus a "stumbling block" or "obstacle." See also 11:6; 13:57; 15:12). A quotation from Zechariah 13:7 that speaks of the disintegration of the community is accompanied by a promise of its renewal. Galilee is the place where Jesus first gathered disciples (4:18-22) and commissioned them (10:1-42) and where he appears to them for the last time, sending them to the whole world (28:16-20). Peter, representative of the whole (see 16:16-23), boasts that this will never happen (vv. 33-35). The irony is strong, as in the next scene the disciples sleep instead of keeping watch (vv. 36-46) and flee (v. 56), while the women disciples stay the course (27:55-56, 61; 28:1-10).

26:36-46 Prayer at Gethsemane

Arriving at Gethsemane (meaning "olive press") with his disciples (v. 36; see 26:20), Jesus separates himself from them to pray, taking along Peter and the sons of Zebedee, namely, James and John. These three were among the first called and sent (4:18-22; 10:2) and were privileged witnesses at the Transfiguration (17:1-8). They are also singled out as the ones who struggled most to understand Jesus' passion (16:22; 20:20-23). The separation of Jesus from the rest of the disciples may be an allusion to Genesis 22:5, where Abraham tells his servants to stay back while he and Isaac pray. While Abraham is exemplary in his faithfulness, he misinterprets what action God desires. Jesus is both faithful to God and understands what action will bring liberation for his people. For him there will be no rescuing angel (26:53).

Three times Jesus implores God to let the cup (a metaphor for death; see 20:22; 26:27) pass from him without drinking it. His grief is extreme (quoting lament psalms 42:4-5; 43:5 at v. 38), and his struggle is real. Jesus is not a puppet in the hand of God. His death is not inevitable. He wrestles with the final choice to proceed with handing over his life.

Jesus' faithfulness in seeking and following God's direction stands in contrast with the

The Betrayal and Arrest of Jesus

[47]While he was still speaking, Judas, one of the Twelve, arrived, accompanied by a large crowd, with swords and clubs, who had come from the chief priests and the elders of the people. [48]His betrayer had arranged a sign with them, saying, "The man I shall kiss is the one; arrest him." [49]Immediately he went over to Jesus and said, "Hail, Rabbi!" and he kissed him. [50]Jesus answered him, "Friend, do what you have come for." Then stepping forward they laid hands on Jesus and arrested him. [51]And behold, one of those who accompanied Jesus put his hand to his sword, drew it, and struck the high priest's servant, cutting off his ear.

continue

frailty of his disciples. They fail to keep watch (see chs. 24–25) and do not pray, as Jesus had instructed (v. 41 and 6:13), to be delivered from the test (*peirasmos*)—both the present crisis and the eschatological trial. Yet they will be restored and empowered by the risen Christ (28:7, 16-20). The final scenes of intimacy between Jesus and his followers began with Jesus noting at the supper that his appointed hour was at hand (26:18). They now close with his declaration that both the hour and the one handing him over are at hand (vv. 45-46).

26:47-56 Jesus' arrest

Jesus' words are immediately fulfilled with the arrival of Judas and a large, armed crowd, who come on the authority of the chief priests and elders. With so many people in the city for the feast, Judas has prearranged a signal so that there will be no confusion. A kiss, normally given by a disciple to a teacher as a sign of respect, turns treacherous. And as at the Last Supper (26:25), Judas addresses Jesus as Rabbi (v. 49), against Jesus' instructions (23:8). The tone of Jesus' response (v. 50) is not clear. It can be understood as an ironic question, "Friend, why are you here?" (KJV) or an instruction that emphasizes Jesus' control of the scene: "Friend,

⁵²Then Jesus said to him, "Put your sword back into its sheath, for all who take the sword will perish by the sword. ⁵³Do you think that I cannot call upon my Father and he will not provide me at this moment with more than twelve legions of angels? ⁵⁴But then how would the scriptures be fulfilled which say that it must come to pass in this way?" ⁵⁵At that hour Jesus said to the crowds, "Have you come out as against a robber, with swords and clubs to seize me? Day after day I sat teaching in the temple area, yet you did not arrest me. ⁵⁶But all this has come to pass that the writings of the prophets may be fulfilled." Then all the disciples left him and fled.

Jesus before the Sanhedrin

⁵⁷Those who had arrested Jesus led him away to Caiaphas the high priest, where the scribes and the elders were assembled. ⁵⁸Peter was following him at a distance as far as the high priest's courtyard, and going inside he sat down with the servants to see the outcome. ⁵⁹The chief priests and the entire Sanhedrin kept trying to obtain false testimony against Jesus in order to put him to death, ⁶⁰but they found none, though many false witnesses came forward. Finally two came forward ⁶¹who stated, "This man said, 'I can destroy the temple of God and within three days rebuild it.'" ⁶²The high priest rose and addressed him,

continue

do what you have come for" (NABRE). Or, by addressing Judas as "friend," he reminds him of their intimate relationship and holds out to him the possibility of forgiveness, recalling that Judas has partaken in the cup of his blood that is shed for forgiveness of sins (26:28).

A desperate attempt on the part of a disciple to halt the arrest (v. 51) serves to underscore once again a lack of understanding. Jesus has taught his followers not to counter violence with violence (5:38-48), which he reinforces here with a pronouncement unique to Matthew: "all who take the sword will perish by the sword" (v. 52; similarly Rev 13:10). More-

over, Jesus withstands the temptation to call upon angelic rescuers (v. 53, as at 4:6). As always, Matthew explains that all these seemingly incomprehensible events happen to fulfill the Scriptures (v. 54, 56). The fallibility of the disciples culminates with their desertion and fleeing (v. 56; but see 27:55-56, 61; 28:1-10, where the Galilean women continue to follow and serve).

26:57-68 Interrogation before the Sanhedrin

The arresting party brings Jesus to the high priest, scribes, and elders (the Pharisees have dropped from view in the passion narrative and only reappear at 27:62). The mention of Peter (v. 58) prepares for the next scene, in which he denies Jesus (vv. 69-75). The Jewish leaders do not have authority to put a person to death (John 18:31). While Matthew gives the scene the aura of a trial, it is more a strategy session to prepare the case they will present to Pilate. In Christian tradition, the blame for Jesus' death increasingly has been taken off the Romans and put on the Jewish leaders. Matthew paints the Jewish leaders as vile, seeking *false* testimony (v. 59; cf. Mark 14:55) against Jesus.

Two witnesses are necessary for a death sentence (Deut 17:6). The accusation that Jesus said he can destroy the temple and rebuild it (v. 61) is both false and ironically correct. Although he performed a prophetic act in judgment on the temple (21:1-17) and remarked about its coming destruction (24:2), he did not say that he himself would destroy it. But since destruction and restoration of the temple were thought to be a sign of the messianic age, the accusation is actually true. Jesus' initial silence toward the high priest (v. 63) recalls that of the servant in Isaiah 53:7. At 27:40 the charge will be made again by passersby reviling the crucified Jesus.

The high priest shifts the focus, demanding that Jesus respond under oath to the charge that he is Messiah, Son of God (v. 64). That Jesus is Messiah has been affirmed from the opening line of the Gospel (1:1, 17, 18; 2:4; 11:2;

16:16; 22:42; 23:10). "Son of God" underscores his unique relationship with God (2:15; 3:17; 11:25-27; 17:5), his healing power (8:29), and his authority (see 14:33; 16:20, where the two titles occur in tandem). Jesus had taught his disciples not to take oaths (7:33-37). He replies to the high priest with the same enigmatic phrase, "You have said so" (v. 64), that he had said to Judas (26:25) and to Pilate (27:11). His further response underscores his identity as the coming Human One. Blending Psalm 110:1 and Daniel 7:13, he moves the discussion to an eschatological plane. At this the high priest accuses Jesus of blasphemy, that is, abusing the divine name or insulting God (v. 65), an offense the leaders deem worthy of death (v. 66). They themselves begin to abuse Jesus (cf. Mark 14:65, where it is an anonymous "some") and mock his identity as prophet and Messiah (vv. 67-68), an element unique to Matthew.

 Peter is the most important of the original twelve apostles. The New Testament shows his prominence in several ways, especially by means of his role as the primary voice of the apostles. Peter uniformly appears first in the lists of the Twelve (Matt 10:2 and parallels), he confessed Jesus as the Messiah (Mark 8:29 and parallels), and he is among the first to encounter the risen Jesus (1 Cor 15:5). While his preeminence is clear, he is also a complex figure whose limitations the New Testament does not hide. Essentially, Peter is both saint and sinner.

26:69-75 Peter denies Jesus

The utter failure of Peter is not unexpected; Jesus has warned that this will happen (26:31-35). Peter has been in the lead as one of the first disciples called (4:18-22) and was a privileged witness at the Transfiguration (17:1-8). He was the spokesperson for the disciples in declaring Jesus "messiah" (16:16), and the one to whom Jesus entrusted the "keys to the kingdom of

"Have you no answer? What are these men testifying against you?" [63]But Jesus was silent. Then the high priest said to him, "I order you to tell us under oath before the living God whether you are the Messiah, the Son of God." [64]Jesus said to him in reply, "You have said so. But I tell you:

From now on you will see 'the Son of Man seated at the right hand of the Power' and 'coming on the clouds of heaven.'"

[65]Then the high priest tore his robes and said, "He has blasphemed! What further need have we of witnesses? You have now heard the blasphemy; [66]what is your opinion?" They said in reply, "He deserves to die!" [67]Then they spat in his face and struck him, while some slapped him, [68]saying, "Prophesy for us, Messiah: who is it that struck you?"

Peter's Denial of Jesus

[69]Now Peter was sitting outside in the courtyard. One of the maids came over to him and said, "You too were with Jesus the Galilean." [70]But he denied it in front of everyone, saying, "I do not know what you are talking about!" [71]As he went out to the gate, another girl saw him and said to those who were there, "This man was with Jesus the Nazorean." [72]Again he denied it with an oath, "I do not know the man!" [73]A little later the

continue

heaven" (16:19). But he has also been the prime example of a disciple who struggles to understand and fails miserably (16:22-23; 26:33-35). Not once but three times he denies being with Jesus, and he does so with an oath (see 5:33-37, where Jesus forbids oath-taking). Matthew adds that Peter makes the denial "in front of everyone" (v. 70; cf. 5:16; 10:32-33). This is the last mention of Peter in Matthew's Gospel. Presumably his bitter tears (v. 75) are tears of repentance, and he is among the disciples to whom the women announce the good news (28:7-10) and among those who are commissioned to preach to all the nations (28:16).

bystanders came over and said to Peter, "Surely you too are one of them; even your speech gives you away." [74]At that he began to curse and to swear, "I do not know the man." And immediately a cock crowed. [75]Then Peter remembered the word that Jesus had spoken: "Before the cock crows you will deny me three times." He went out and began to weep bitterly.

CHAPTER 27

Jesus before Pilate

[1]When it was morning, all the chief priests and the elders of the people took counsel against Jesus to put him to death. [2]They bound him, led him away, and handed him over to Pilate, the governor.

The Death of Judas

[3]Then Judas, his betrayer, seeing that Jesus had been condemned, deeply regretted what he had done. He returned the thirty pieces of silver to the chief priests and elders, [4]saying, "I have sinned in betraying innocent blood." They said, "What is that to us? Look to it yourself." [5]Flinging the money into the temple, he departed and went off and hanged himself. [6]The chief priests gathered up the money, but said, "It is not lawful to deposit this in the temple treasury, for it is the price of blood." [7]After consultation, they used it to buy the potter's field as a burial place for foreigners. [8]That is why that field even today is called the Field of Blood. [9]Then was fulfilled what had been said through Jeremiah the prophet, "And they took the thirty pieces of silver, the value of a man with a price on his head, a price set by some of the

continue

27:1-2 The council hands Jesus over

After a night of interrogation and abuse, the chief priests and elders fulfill what Jesus had predicted at 20:18-19. They hand Jesus over (*paradidōmi*, 10:4; 26:15, 25; 27:3, 18, 26) to the Roman governor, Pontius Pilate, who ruled from A.D. 26 to 36.

27:3-10 The death of Judas

Seeing Jesus condemned prompts a change of heart in Judas. Ordinarily the verb *metanoein* is used for repentance, whereas here it is *metameletheis*, "deeply regretted" (v. 3). But it is likely that Judas' words in verse 4 indicate true repentance and not simply regret. Judas, like the leaders Jesus warned in 23:35-36, is responsible for shedding innocent blood. (See 27:24, where Pilate will try to make himself innocent of Jesus' blood.) The leaders dissociate themselves from Judas' attempt to return the money (see 27:24 for Pilate's use of the same phrase, "Look to it yourselves"). In desperation, Judas flings the money into the temple and tragically ends his life. A rather different version is found in Acts 1:15-20. The quotation in verses 9-10 interpreting the purchase of the "Field of Blood" is actually an adaptation of Zechariah 11:12-13, although Matthew attributes it to Jeremiah. Perhaps Matthew makes the association because of a similarity with the slaughter of the innocents (2:17-18), interpreted with Jeremiah 31:15. Or Matthew may mean to recall Jesus' critique of the temple and its leadership (21:13, quoting Jer 7:11). Alternatively, he may be alluding to the story of the potter's field in Jeremiah 18–19.

27:11-14 Trial before Pilate

Resuming the action begun at verse 2, Matthew now tells of the interrogation by the Roman governor. His question is different from that of the Jewish authorities and concerns Jesus' kingship. Once again Jesus answers enigmatically, "You say so" (v. 11; see 26:64), and then remains silent when the chief priests and elders testify against him (as also 26:63). Jesus' silence is evocative again of the servant of Isaiah 53:7, whose appearance caused amazement (Isa 52:14-15; v. 14).

27:15-26 Choice of Barabbas

Beyond the Gospel references, there is no other evidence of a custom of releasing a prisoner at Passover. The choice, according to Matthew, is between Jesus Barabbas and "Jesus called Messiah" (v. 17). Matthew heightens the notoriety of the former (v. 16) and names envy as the motive for handing Jesus over (v. 18). Three other unique elements in Matthew serve to shift the blame away from Pilate and onto the Jewish leaders. The first is the dream of Pilate's wife, who urges her husband to "have nothing to do with that righteous man" (v. 19). In the opening chapters, dreams are the means by which Joseph, a "righteous man" (1:19), learns God's desire and by what actions he is to preserve the life of Jesus and his mother (1:20; 2:13, 19, 22). A second element found only in Matthew is Pilate's handwashing (v. 24), a futile attempt to declare his own innocence and to dissociate himself from Jesus' death (similarly the chief priests with Judas, 27:4). A third unique feature of the Matthean account is the climactic cry of the whole people, "His blood be upon us and upon our children" (v. 25).

Until this point the crowds have been basically favorable toward Jesus. Now they demand his crucifixion (vv. 22, 23), and the people as a whole (*laos*, as at 1:21) take upon themselves the responsibility for his blood (v. 25; see Lev 20:9-16; Josh 2:19-20; 2 Sam 1:16; 14:9; Jer 51:35). This verse has been interpreted as a curse upon all Jewish people for all time. This is a grave misinterpretation that Christians have a serious obligation to counter (see the Vatican II document *Nostra Aetate* 4). In the context of Matthew's Gospel, "the whole people" refers to those who opposed Jesus during his lifetime as well as Jewish opponents of the early Christian community. Verse 25 reflects the inner family conflict and the struggle of Jesus' disciples to understand why all Jews did not follow Jesus (similarly Matthew 13; Romans 9–11). Matthew sees a connection between the rejection of Jesus and the events that unfold in the decades following Jesus' death ("upon our children"), particularly the destruction of the temple. The scene concludes with Pilate releasing Barabbas, having Jesus scourged to weaken him, and handing him over (*paradidōmi*, 10:4; 20:18; 26:15, 25; 27:2, 3, 18, 26) for the last time to the soldiers to crucify him.

Israelites, [10]and they paid it out for the potter's field just as the Lord had commanded me."

Jesus Questioned by Pilate

[11]Now Jesus stood before the governor, and he questioned him, "Are you the king of the Jews?" Jesus said, "You say so." [12]And when he was accused by the chief priests and elders, he made no answer. [13]Then Pilate said to him, "Do you not hear how many things they are testifying against you?" [14]But he did not answer him one word, so that the governor was greatly amazed.

The Sentence of Death

[15]Now on the occasion of the feast the governor was accustomed to release to the crowd one prisoner whom they wished. [16]And at that time they had a notorious prisoner called [Jesus] Barabbas. [17]So when they had assembled, Pilate said to them, "Which one do you want me to release to you, [Jesus] Barabbas, or Jesus called Messiah?" [18]For he knew that it was out of envy that they had handed him over. [19]While he was still seated on the bench, his wife sent him a message, "Have nothing to do with that righteous man. I suffered much in a dream today because of him." [20]The chief priests and the elders persuaded the crowds to ask for Barabbas but to destroy Jesus. [21]The governor said to them in reply, "Which of the two do you want me to release to you?" They answered, "Barabbas!" [22]Pilate said to them, "Then what shall I do with Jesus called Messiah?" They all said, "Let him be crucified!" [23]But he said, "Why? What evil has he done?" They only shouted the louder, "Let him be crucified!" [24]When Pilate saw that he was not succeeding at all, but that a riot was breaking out instead, he took water and washed his hands in the sight of the crowd, saying, "I am innocent of this man's blood. Look to it yourselves." [25]And the whole people said in reply, "His blood be upon us and upon our children." [26]Then he released Barabbas to them, but after he had Jesus scourged, he handed him over to be crucified.

continue

Mockery by the Soldiers

²⁷Then the soldiers of the governor took Jesus inside the praetorium and gathered the whole cohort around him. ²⁸They stripped off his clothes and threw a scarlet military cloak about him. ²⁹Weaving a crown out of thorns, they placed it on his head, and a reed in his right hand. And kneeling before him, they mocked him, saying, "Hail, King of the Jews!" ³⁰They spat upon him and took the reed and kept striking him on the head. ³¹And when they had mocked him, they stripped him of the cloak, dressed him in his own clothes, and led him off to crucify him.

The Way of the Cross

³²As they were going out, they met a Cyrenian named Simon; this man they pressed into service to carry his cross.

The Crucifixion

³³And when they came to a place called Golgotha (which means Place of the Skull), ³⁴they gave Jesus wine to drink mixed with gall. But when he had tasted it, he refused to drink. ³⁵After they had crucified him, they divided his garments by casting lots; ³⁶then they sat down and kept watch over him there. ³⁷And they placed over his head the written charge against him: This is Jesus, the King of the Jews. ³⁸Two revolutionaries were crucified with him, one on his right and the other on his left. ³⁹Those passing by reviled him, shaking their heads ⁴⁰and saying, "You who would destroy the temple and rebuild it in three days, save yourself, if you are the Son of God, [and] come down from the cross!" ⁴¹Likewise the chief priests with the scribes and elders mocked him and said, ⁴²"He saved others; he cannot save himself. So he is the king of Israel! Let him come down from the cross now, and we will believe in him. ⁴³He trusted in God; let him deliver him now if he wants him. For he said, 'I am the Son of God.'" ⁴⁴The revolutionaries who were crucified with him also kept abusing him in the same way.

continue

27:27-31 Mockery by the soldiers

Just as the interrogation before the chief priests and elders ended with them abusing Jesus (26:67-68), so the Roman trial concludes with abuse by the soldiers of the governor inside the praetorium, the governor's official residence. A cohort consisted of six hundred men; in verse 27 it likely refers to simply a large group of soldiers. These would have been local men employed by the Romans. They mock Jesus' kingship, arraying him in scarlet, with a pseudo-crown and scepter. In Mark 15:17 the robe is purple, a color worn by royalty and the rich (see, e.g., Luke 16:19), but Matthew's detail is more realistic. Roman soldiers wore red cloaks; they simply adorn Jesus in one of their own. The crown of thorns was not so much to inflict pain as to imitate that of an emperor with its rays. The acclamation (v. 29) simulates the greeting toward the emperor, "Ave, Caesar!" The derisive mockery turns to physical abuse (v. 30) and ends with Jesus being led to crucifixion.

27:32 Simon of Cyrene

On the way to the site of crucifixion, Simon of Cyrene (a North African city in present-day Libya) is pressed into service to help Jesus carry the cross. Likely he was visiting Jerusalem for the Passover feast. While Jesus has said that those who wish to be his follower must take up their cross (16:24), discipleship motifs are not entirely clear in this scene, especially since Simon is forced into carrying the crossbeam. At the same time, the presence of this Simon is a poignant reminder of the absence of Simon Peter, who has struggled to accept the fact that Jesus would die (16:21-23), then declared he would follow Jesus to the death (26:33-35), but has fled (26:56) and denied that he was ever with Jesus (26:69-75).

27:33-44 Crucifixion and mockery

The place of crucifixion, Golgotha, "Place of the Skull," gets its name either because the hill is skull-shaped or because of the executions that took place there. It was customary to give the condemned person a drink mixed with a narcotic to ease the pain. Matthew makes it wine mixed with gall, so that the action corresponds to what is said in Psalm 69:21.

The title **"King of the Jews"** is curious in that it represents an "outsider's" perspective. The normal title for a Davidic king is "King of Israel." But Alexander Jannaeus (103–76 B.C.) and Herod the Great (37–4 B.C.), neither of whom was Davidic, both possessed the title "King of the Jews" when they ruled Palestine. An archaeological find in 1996 confirmed the title for Herod the Great when an inscription was discovered on a clay wine jug at a 2,000-year-old garbage dump at Masada in Israel. This fact makes the passion narratives of the Gospels all the more comprehensible. Jesus may have been crucified for political reasons as a threat to Roman authority for trying, in their view, to reestablish a Jewish monarchy.

No details are narrated about the crucifixion itself (v. 35). Matthew's readers are well familiar with what other contemporary writers describe as the most cruel and painful of all punishments. It was used on slaves, violent criminals, and political rebels. Carried out in a public place, it was meant to be a deterrent. Matthew focuses on how to make meaning of this horrible death. He uses the Scriptures, primarily the lament psalms, to interpret each action. In verse 35 the division of Jesus' clothing alludes to Psalm 22:18. The wagging heads of the mockers (v. 39) recalls Psalm 22:7.

For the third time (26:67-68; 27:27-31) Jesus endures mockery. First the passersby (vv. 39-40) resurrect the charge made before the Sanhedrin (26:61) about the destruction of the temple, an event that Matthew connects with the death of Jesus (21:41, 43). Their taunt, "If you are the Son of God," recalls the same tempting words of Satan (4:3, 6), who urges Jesus to throw himself from the pinnacle of the

The Death of Jesus

[45]From noon onward, darkness came over the whole land until three in the afternoon. [46]And about three o'clock Jesus cried out in a loud voice, *"Eli, Eli, lema sabachthani?"* which means, "My God, my God, why have you forsaken me?" [47]Some of the bystanders who heard it said, "This one is calling for Elijah." [48]Immediately one of them ran to get a sponge; he soaked it in wine, and putting it on a reed, gave it to him to drink. [49]But the rest said, "Wait, let us see if Elijah comes to save him." [50]But Jesus cried out again in a loud voice, and gave up his spirit. [51]And behold, the

continue

temple and let God's angels rescue him to prove he is truly God's Son. Both scenes reflect the struggle of believers to explain how Jesus can be the beloved Son of God (2:15; 3:17; 17:5) and yet die such a horrendous death. The taunt of the chief priests, scribes, and elders is a variation of the same (vv. 41-42). The paradox of saving life by losing life (16:25) is visibly played out. It is through losing his life that Jesus "saves his people from their sins" (1:21). While the placard over the cross (v. 37) carries the title "King of the Jews" (the charge made by Pilate, 27:11, and his soldiers, 27:29), the religious leaders use the more messianically charged phrase "King of Israel" (v. 42). Verse 43, unique to Matthew, employs Psalm 22:9 and Wisdom 2:18 to align Jesus with the righteous sufferer whom God will vindicate. Finally, even the bandits crucified with Jesus join in the abuse (v. 44; cf. Luke 23:40-43).

27:45-56 Death of Jesus

An apocalyptic tone is set as darkness spreads over the land for three hours (see Amos 8:9). Jesus cries out in a loud voice (v. 46), once again using the words of Psalm 22. He has been deserted and opposed by Judas (26:14-16, 48-49), the disciples (26:56), Peter (26:69-75), the religious leaders (26:57-68), the veil of the sanctuary was torn in two from top to bottom. The earth quaked, rocks were split, [52]tombs were opened, and the bodies of many saints who had fallen asleep were raised. [53]And coming forth from their tombs after his resurrection, they entered the holy city and appeared to many. [54]The centurion and the men with him who were keeping watch over Jesus feared greatly when they saw the earthquake and all that was happening, and they said, "Truly, this was the Son of God!" [55]There were many women there, looking on from a distance, who had followed Jesus from Galilee, ministering to him. [56]Among them were Mary Magdalene and Mary the mother of James and Joseph, and the mother of the sons of Zebedee.

continue

crowds (27:21-22), the Roman authorities (27:1-31), and now even God seems to have abandoned him. His anguished prayer is that of a righteous sufferer. While the end of the psalm, which moves to a note of confident hope in God's power to save, is not spoken, the Gospel will indeed end with Jesus' vindication.

The bystanders either misinterpret or deliberately mock Jesus (v. 47) and think he is calling on Elijah. There was an expectation that Elijah would return before the final judgment (Mal 4:5; Sir 48:10). But John the Baptist has already played this role (Matt 11:14; 17:10-13). It is not entirely clear what prompts the offer of *oxos*, a cheap, sour wine used by the lower classes (v. 48), or whether this is a compassionate or mocking gesture. Most likely Matthew includes it as one more way in which Scriptures (Ps 69:21) are fulfilled. As terse as the notice of Jesus' crucifixion (v. 35) is the statement he "gave up his spirit" (v. 50). This is not a reference to the Holy Spirit but to the life-breath (*pneuma* means both "spirit" and "breath") that Jesus hands back to God. Matthew portrays Jesus not as an unwilling victim but as faithful Son of God who consciously returns to God.

Four apocalyptic signs follow immediately, powerful demonstrations that God did not abandon Jesus:

1) The curtain of the temple, probably the inner veil in front of the holy of holies (Exod 26:31-35), is torn (the passive voice designates this as God's doing) from top to bottom. This can be understood as a portent of the destruction of the temple or as opening access to the God of Israel to all the Gentiles.

2) The earthquakes, a portent of the end of the present age and the beginning of the new (4 Ezra 6:13-16; 2 *Apoc. Bar.* 27:7; 70:8; Zech 14:4-5; Matt 24:7). Cosmic signs accompany the momentous events of Jesus' birth (2:2), his death, his resurrection (28:2), and his return in glory (24:27-31).

3) Many of the holy dead emerge from their tombs and appear to people in Jerusalem (vv. 52-53). In verse 52, Matthew, in language akin to that of Ezekiel 37, asserts that it is Jesus' death that makes possible the resurrection of the holy ones. The sequence of events becomes confused in verse 53 because Matthew makes a correction: the resurrection of others cannot happen until the resurrection of Jesus, which Matthew has not yet narrated.

4) The centurion and those with him, who had participated in crucifying Jesus, come to believe in Jesus and declare, "Truly this was the Son of God!" (v. 54; cf. vv. 40, 43). This is all the more significant when their employer, the emperor, allocated this title to himself, seeing himself as agent of the gods.

Not only has God not abandoned Jesus but the many Galilean women disciples have also remained faithful to him (vv. 55-56). They are steadfastly keeping watch (as Jesus exhorts disciples to do in chapters 24–25), after having followed Jesus from Galilee and having ministered (*diakonousai*) to him (see 8:15 for various meanings of this verb). Mary Magdalene heads the list (v. 56; as in Matt 27:61; 28:1; Mark 15:40, 47; 16:1, 9; Luke 8:2; 24:10; cf. John 19:25; 20:1-2, 11-18). No information is given about her before this point in the narrative. Only Luke 8:2-3 introduces her before the passion account. The common confusion of her with a prostitute or a sinner has no basis in the Scriptures. The other Mary accompanying her is the mother of James and Joseph (cf. Mark 15:40). At Matthew 13:55 there is the mention of Jesus having siblings named James and Joseph. Possibly Matthew is alluding to the mother of Jesus (cf. John 19:25), but if so, he does not develop the significance. The third figure is the mother of the sons of Zebedee, who at 20:20-21 had wanted places of honor for her sons in Jesus' realm. She drops out of the list in 27:61 and 28:1.

27:57-66 Witnesses at the tomb

Another disciple emerges, a rich man (see 19:16-26, where Jesus elaborates on how difficult it is for a rich person to be a disciple) who offers his tomb for Jesus' burial. There is no mention of Joseph having been part of the Sanhedrin that condemned Jesus (cf. Mark 14:53). There are many limestone quarries in Jerusalem, some of which were used secondarily as cemeteries. A body would be laid in a niche carved in the rock until the flesh decomposed. Then the bones would be gathered into an ossuary ("bone box"), and the niche could be reused for another family member. A tomb complex would have a number of niches. The stone is rolled across the entrance to prevent grave robbers or animals from entering. No anointing of Jesus' body is narrated, since he has already been anointed for burial by an unnamed woman (26:6-13).

Keeping vigil at the tomb (v. 61) are Mary Magdalene and the "other Mary," presumably the mother of James and Joseph named in verse 56. They come again in 28:1 to see the tomb. These witnesses serve to verify that Jesus is truly dead and that there is no mistaking the place of his burial.

Unique to Matthew is the request of the chief priests and the Pharisees (who have been absent since 23:39) to Pilate to set a guard at the tomb (vv. 62-66). Their recollection of Jesus' prediction that after three days he would rise (16:21; 17:23; 20:19) sets the stage for the empty tomb and the resurrection appearances. Their fear of the impact of the disciples' proclamation that Jesus was raised from the dead (v. 64)

The Burial of Jesus

[57]When it was evening, there came a rich man from Arimathea named Joseph, who was himself a disciple of Jesus. [58]He went to Pilate and asked for the body of Jesus; then Pilate ordered it to be handed over. [59]Taking the body, Joseph wrapped it [in] clean linen [60]and laid it in his new tomb that he had hewn in the rock. Then he rolled a huge stone across the entrance to the tomb and departed. [61]But Mary Magdalene and the other Mary remained sitting there, facing the tomb.

The Guard at the Tomb

[62]The next day, the one following the day of preparation, the chief priests and the Pharisees gathered before Pilate [63]and said, "Sir, we remember that this impostor while still alive said, 'After three days I will be raised up.' [64]Give orders, then, that the grave be secured until the third day, lest his disciples come and steal him and say to the people, 'He has been raised from the dead.' This last imposture would be worse than the first." [65]Pilate said to them, "The guard is yours; go secure it as best you can." [66]So they went and secured the tomb by fixing a seal to the stone and setting the guard.

CHAPTER 28

The Resurrection of Jesus

[1]After the sabbath, as the first day of the week was dawning, Mary Magdalene and the other Mary came to see the tomb. [2]And behold, there

continue

is ironic, since this is exactly what occurs. The charge that Jesus was an "imposter" (v. 63) and that his disciples stole the body (v. 64) likely reflects the kinds of arguments Matthew's community encountered from their opponents.

28:1-15 The empty tomb

The same two women who witnessed Jesus' crucifixion (27:55-56) and who kept vigil at his burial (27:61) return once again to the tomb. As was a great earthquake; for an angel of the Lord descended from heaven, approached, rolled back the stone, and sat upon it. ³His appearance was like lightning and his clothing was white as snow. ⁴The guards were shaken with fear of him and became like dead men. ⁵Then the angel said to the women in reply, "Do not be afraid! I know that you are seeking Jesus the crucified. ⁶He is not here, for he has been raised just as he said. Come and see the place where he lay. ⁷Then go quickly and tell his disciples, 'He has been raised from the dead, and he is going before you to Galilee; there you will see him.' Behold, I have told you." ⁸Then they went away quickly from the tomb, fearful yet overjoyed, and ran to announce this to his disciples. ⁹And behold, Jesus met them on their way and greeted them. They approached, embraced his feet, and did him homage. ¹⁰Then Jesus said to them, "Do not be afraid. Go tell my brothers to go to Galilee, and there they will see me."

The Report of the Guard

¹¹While they were going, some of the guard went into the city and told the chief priests all that had happened. ¹²They assembled with the elders and took counsel; then they gave a large sum of money to the soldiers, ¹³telling them, "You are to say, 'His disciples came by night and stole him while we were asleep.' ¹⁴And if this gets to the ears of the governor, we will satisfy [him] and keep you out of trouble." ¹⁵The soldiers took the money and did as they were instructed. And this story has circulated among the Jews to the present [day].

continue

at the death of Jesus, an earthquake (27:51, 54; see also 24:7), an apocalyptic sign, occurs, accompanied by the descent of an angel from heaven. In the opening chapters an angel conveyed to Joseph the divine interpretation of the puzzling events surrounding Jesus' birth. Similarly, an angel communicates the meaning of the extraordinary aftermath of Jesus' death. In

an ironic play on words and images, the guards who were supposed to secure the dead body, themselves become like dead men (v. 4).

The angel assures the women not to fear and announces that Jesus has been raised as he said (16:21; 17:22-23; 20:18-19). The passive voice "he has been raised" (v. 6) connotes that God performs the action. The angel then commissions the women to go quickly to give the message to the disciples and to instruct them to go to Galilee, where they will see him (fulfilling Jesus' words in 26:32). Matthew does not explicitly mention Peter (cf. Mark 16:7; Luke 24:12, 34), though he is presumably among the disciples (v. 7) and the Eleven (v. 16). The women do exactly as instructed; with fear and great joy, they run to announce the message to the disciples (v. 8; cf. Mark 16:8, where they say nothing because of their fear).

Unique to Matthew are verses 9-10, where Jesus meets the women on the way. That they seize his feet is a detail that attests to the reality of his person and his tangibility. He is not a ghost or a spirit; nor is it simply the memory of Jesus that lives on with them. The women worship (*proskynein*) Jesus (see also 2:8, 11; 14:33; 15:25; 28:17). Jesus' repetition in verse 10 of the message they have already received from the angel (v. 7) is significant in that the women are commissioned directly by Jesus, giving them credentials as prime witnesses and apostles. Matthew's account represents a strand of Christian tradition in the same line as that of John 20:1-2, 11-18, where Mary Magdalene goes to the tomb alone and there encounters the risen Christ and is commissioned to announce the good news to the community of brothers and sisters (20:17). By contrast, in Mark 16:1-8 and Luke 24:1-12 the women do not encounter Jesus but only the angel. Peter is given primacy of place by Luke (24:12, 34) and Paul, who does not list the women among those to whom the risen Christ appeared (1 Cor 15:3-8).

Rounding out the story of the guard at the tomb (27:62-66) is their report to the chief priests of all that had happened (28:11-15). Along with the elders, they gather and take counsel (as 27:1). Just as money figured in the plan to hand Jesus over to death (26:14-16; 27:3-10), so did money figure in the false interpretation of his resurrection (v. 12; see 6:19-34; 10:8-9; 13:22; 19:16-30 for warnings about the dangers of money). The ongoing polemics into Matthew's day between followers of Jesus and their opponents are reflected in the remark in verse 15.

FINALE: BACK TO GALILEE; COMMISSION TO THE WHOLE WORLD; JESUS' ABIDING PRESENCE

Matthew 28:16-20

28:16-20 The Great Commission

In a scene unique to Matthew, the thread of the story of the women's witness, which left off at verse 10, is resumed. It presumes that they have fulfilled their commission to tell the news of the resurrection to the other disciples and that these have believed them. The juxtaposition of "eleven" with "disciples" creates a tension in the narrative. "Eleven" is a reminder that one of "the Twelve" (see 10:1-4) is no more. Yet "the disciples" (referred to seventy-three times in Matthew) comprised a group larger than the Twelve, among whom were most notably the Galilean women who followed and ministered (27:55). While Matthew has depicted the women as apostles who are commissioned in 28:7-10, he excludes them from the commission to preach to all the nations.

The mountaintop setting (as at 4:8; 5:1; 15:29; 17:1) evokes the image of Jesus as the new Moses. Like the women (28:9), the Eleven worship Jesus, though unlike them, they (it is not clear in the Greek whether it is all or some of them) doubt or hesitate before the challenge (*distazō*, v. 17; also 14:31). Until this point in the

The Commissioning of the Disciples

[16]The eleven disciples went to Galilee, to the mountain to which Jesus had ordered them. [17]When they saw him, they worshiped, but they doubted. [18]Then Jesus approached and said to them, "All power in heaven and on earth has been given to me. [19]Go, therefore, and make disciples of all nations, baptizing them in the name of the Father, and of the Son, and of the holy Spirit, [20]teaching them to observe all that I have commanded you. And behold, I am with you always, until the end of the age."

Gospel, Jesus had insisted that the mission was restricted to the "lost sheep of the house of Israel" (10:6; 15:24); now the disciples are to go to "all nations" (*panta ta ethnē*, v. 19; see 25:32). Some understand Matthew to be saying that the mission is to be directed from now on to the Gentiles exclusively (i.e., that the mission to Israel has ended). But more likely Matthew's heavily Jewish Christian community sees that Israel is still included among "all [the] nations" to whom they reach out. The mission is to make disciples, to baptize, and to teach.

A liturgical formula from early Christian tradition has been placed on Jesus' lips (v. 19). As Jesus has been depicted as Teacher par excellence, so are his disciples to follow in his footsteps with his authority (v. 18; see 10:1).

The final verse of the Gospel reiterates the assurance given at 1:23 and 18:20: despite the "little faith" and the failures of his followers, Jesus remains always with the community that gathers and ministers in his name. Not even death can break that bond—ever.

EXPLORING LESSON FOUR

1. a) How do the actions of the woman with the costly oil cast her in a role that is both prophetic and priestly (26:6-13)? (See also 1 Sam 16:12-13; 1 Kgs 1:39.)

_____

_____

_____

_____

_____

   b) How does the woman's anointing of Jesus for burial contrast with the response of Jesus' disciples to the predictions of his death? (See 16:21-23; 17:22-23; 20:17-28.)

_____

_____

_____

_____

_____

2. After a careful reading of Matthew 26:17-35 and the accompanying commentary, what is something new that you learned about the Last Supper?

_____

_____

_____

_____

_____

_____

3. At Gethsemane, Jesus struggles with his own will *versus* the will of God (26:39, 42, 44). Have you ever experienced this kind of struggle? Did the "cup pass" or were you given the strength to "drink" it?

_____

_____

_____

_____

_____

_____

4. Jesus calls Judas "friend" even as Judas comes to betray him (26:50). What does this tell us about both the gravity of Judas' decision and Jesus' attitude toward Judas?

_____

_____

_____

_____

_____

_____

5. Compare Judas' deep regret for what he has done (27:3-5) with Peter's response to his denials of Jesus (26:75). Do you think both responses show repentance?

_____

_____

_____

_____

_____

_____

6. When Jesus is questioned by both the high priest and Pilate, Matthew tells us that Jesus responds with silence (26:63; 27:14). Reflect on the silence of Jesus. Is there power in silence? How is this response in keeping with the nature of Jesus' ministry (e.g., the silence of the seed in Matt 13:31-32)?

_____

_____

_____

_____

_____

7. Matthew 27:25 has sometimes been used to justify anti-Semitism. Why is this inappropriate?

_____

_____

_____

_____

_____

8. a) The commentary makes several connections between the crucifixion of Jesus and Psalm 22. Read Psalm 22. What parallels do you find?

_____

_____

_____

_____

_____

_____

b) How does Psalm 22 end? How does this foreshadow the end of the Gospel (28:6)?

_____

_____

_____

_____

_____

9. a) In the brief account of the women encountering the risen Jesus, what is the significance of them embracing his feet (28:9-10)?

_____

_____

_____

_____

_____

b) What is the significance of Jesus repeating the angel's command that the women should tell his disciples that he has been raised and to meet him in Galilee?

_____

_____

_____

_____

_____

10. How does the risen Christ's commission to the disciples present a major shift in missionary focus (28:16-20)? (See 10:6; 15:24.) When have you felt called to move beyond what is expected or comfortable?

_____

_____

_____

_____

_____

_____

CLOSING PRAYER

Prayer

"Truly, this was the Son of God!"
(Matt 27:54)

Jesus Christ, Son of God, we have come to know you in the words of this Gospel and in our time spent together in a spirit of discipleship. May the words we have read and the study we have undertaken continue to bless us as individuals and as a church so we may follow your command to go out into the world bearing your good news. We will carry with us in spirit and in prayer those most in need of your ongoing presence, especially . . .

PRAYING WITH YOUR GROUP

Because we know that the Bible allows us to hear God's voice, prayer provides the context for our study and sharing. By speaking and listening to God and each other, the discussion often grows to more deeply bond us to one another and to God.

At *the beginning and end of each lesson* simple prayers are provided for individual use, and also may be used within the group setting. Most of the closing prayers provided with each lesson relate directly to a theme from that lesson and encourage you to pray together for people and events in your local community.

Of course, there are many ways to center ourselves in God's presence as we gather together in groups around the word of God. We provide some additional suggestions here knowing you and your group will make prayer a priority as part of your gathering. These are simply alternative ways to pray if your group would like to try something different from those prayers provided in the previous pages.

Conversational Prayer

This form of prayer allows for the group members to pray in their own words in a way that is not intimidating. The group leader begins with Step One, inviting all to focus on the presence of Christ among them. After a few moments of quiet, the group leader invites anyone in the group to voice a prayer or two of thanksgiving; once that is complete, then anyone who has personal intentions may pray in their own words for their needs; finally, the group prays for the needs of others.

A suggested process:
In your own words, speak simple and short prayers to allow time for others to add their voices.

Focus on one "step" at a time, not worrying about praying for everything in your mental list at once.

Step One	Visualize Christ. Welcome him. Imagine him present with you in your group. Allow time for some silence.
Step Two	Gratitude opens our hearts. Use simple words such as, "Thank you, Lord, for . . ."
Step Three	Pray for your own needs knowing that others will pray with you. Be specific and honest. Use "I" and "me" language.

Step Four	Pray for others by name, with love.
	You may voice your agreement ("Yes, Lord").
	End with gratitude for sharing concerns.

Praying Like Ignatius

St. Ignatius Loyola, whose life and ministry are the foundation of the Jesuit community, invites us to enter into Scripture texts in order to experience the scenes, especially scenes of the gospels or other narrative parts of Scripture. Simply put, this is a method of creatively imagining the scene, viewing it from the inside, and asking God to meet you there. Most often, this is a personal form of prayer but in a group setting, some of its elements can be helpful if you allow time for this process.

A suggested process:

- Select a scene from the chapters in the particular lesson.
- Read that scene out loud in the group, followed by some quiet time.
- Ask group members to place themselves in the scene (as a character, or as an onlooker) so that they can imagine the emotions, responses, and thinking that may have taken place. Notice the details and the tone, and imagine the interaction with the Lord that is taking place.
- Share with the group any insights that came to you in this quiet imagining.
- Allow each person in the group to thank God for some insight and to pray about some request that may have surfaced.

Sacred Reading (or Lectio Divina)

This method of prayer invites us to "listen with the ear of the heart" as St. Benedict's rule would say. We listen to the words and the phrasing, asking God to speak to our innermost being. Again, this method of prayer is most often used in an individual setting but may also be used in an adapted way within a group.

A suggested process:

- Select a scene from the chapters in the particular lesson.
- Read the scene out loud in the group, perhaps two times.
- Ask group members to ponder a word or phrase that stands out to them.
- The group members could then simply speak the word or phrase as a kind of litany of what was meaningful for your group.
- Allow time for more silence to ponder the words that were heard, asking God to reveal to you what message you are meant to hear, how God is speaking to you.
- Follow up with spoken intentions at the close of this group time.

REFLECTING ON SCRIPTURE

Reading Scripture is an opportunity not simply to learn new information but to listen to God who loves you. Pray that the same Holy Spirit who guided the formation of Scripture will inspire you to correctly understand what you read, and empower you to make what you read a part of your life.

The inspired word of God contains layers of meaning. As you make your way through passages of Scripture, whether studying a book of the Bible or focusing on a biblical theme, you may find it helpful to ask yourself these four questions:

What does the Scripture passage say?
Read the passage slowly and reflectively. Become familiar with it. If the passage you are reading is a narrative, carefully observe the characters and the plot. Use your imagination to picture the scene or enter into it.

What does the Scripture passage mean?
Read the footnotes in your Bible and the commentary provided to help you understand what the sacred writers intended and what God wants to communicate by means of their words.

What does the Scripture passage mean to me?
Meditate on the passage. God's word is living and powerful. What is God saying to you? How does the Scripture passage apply to your life today?

What am I going to do about it?
Try to discover how God may be challenging you in this passage. An encounter with God contains a challenge to know God's will and follow it more closely in daily life. Ask the Holy Spirit to inspire not only your mind but your life with this living word.